D0065673

ALWAYS ENOUGH THYME

FABULOUS FIVE INC

STEPHANIE McKEE   PHYLLIS JONES

DEBBIE RUBIN   JAN TONROY   DIANE EARL

Published by
Fabulous Five, Inc.
Authors: Stephanie McKee, Diane Earl, Debbie Rubin,
Phyllis Jones, Jan Tonroy
P.O. Box 1068
Aledo, Texas 76008
Fax: (817) 441-5012
Email address: Fabfive54321@aol.com
Web address: thefabulousfive.com

First Printing   April 2001
5,000 copies
Second Printing   September 2001
5,000 copies
Third Printing   July 2003
5,000 copies

Copyright © 2001
By Fabulous Five, Inc. All rights reserved
ISBN 0-9709147-0-9
Library of Congress Number: 2001088041

All Rights Reserved. No part of this book may be reproduced in
any form without written permission from the publishers, except
for brief passages included in a review appearing in a newspaper
or magazine with permission from the publisher.

Manufactured by
Favorite Recipes® Press
an imprint of
FRP
P.O. Box 305142
Nashville, Tennessee 37230
800-358-0560

GREETINGS

The Fabulous Five:
Stephanie McKee, Diane Earl, Debbie Rubin, Phyllis Jones, Jan Tonroy

This cookbook began when four of us (Jan, Debbie, Stephanie and Phyllis) realized we enjoyed each other's company so much we would take turns hosting a monthly dinner entertainment in our homes. From our very first cooking event in September of 1987, we saved the recipes and the menu. For the second dinner in October, we all dressed in Halloween costumes to add a special flourish to the evening, and again, we saved the recipes and the menu. It was at this first Halloween event that Debbie invited Diane, who had been her college roommate, and the Fabulous Five was born.

What began as a monthly "girls' night out" in Lubbock, Texas, has blossomed into a major cooking, traveling, and sharing extravaganza that takes place ritualistically in Lubbock and also in Fort Worth, Texas, where Debbie and Jan now live, as well as other places on spring trips and fall retreats. For fourteen years now, we have supported each other through births, divorces, deaths, promotions, resignations, illnesses, and all the other highs and lows of life, as heart's core companions who consider the preparing and presentation of delicious food a vital part of our deep and joyous relationship.

Our friendship was born around the dining room table, and from the beginning, we've saved all of the recipes that have played such an important part of our fellowship. We are pleased to share them with you in this cookbook, presented in menu format as a completely planned dining experience poised for the making.

ACKNOWLEDGMENTS

We would like to thank our husbands and children
for their love, support, and good appetites.
We would also like to thank our friends for
their encouragement and their contribution of
special recipes to our book.

DEDICATION

To our sweet friend

DEBBIE POWELL RUBIN

She has faced and overcome breast cancer
with a style, courage, and grace
that has taught the rest of us
the healing power of love and faith.

CONTENTS

This cookbook offers all of the delicious recipes from our many cooperative dinners, as well as menu planning, themed meals, our own "Fabulous Footnotes," and general information we want to share. The collection represents the evolution of our friendship. We have always prepared meals to please each other, and these menus reflect our shared appreciation of interesting tastes and surprising combinations. They also reflect our West Texas roots and our close kinship with the Great American Southwest.

To us, green chiles, corn bread, and guacamole are staples, and they appear in a number of renditions throughout the book. Of course, West Texas is quintessential cattle country, and we are delighted to share many menus featuring beef tenderloin, steak, roast, and hamburger. Lastly, however, these menus represent our taste for the sumptuous over the smoldering and the surprising over the standard. They have been compiled as a memorable collection of dishes to stimulate conversation and close companionship.

RISE 'N SHINE

You are never too old for a Slumber party!
Fab Five

RISE 'N SHINE

When Stephanie had her second child in 1988, we started a special tradition. Instead of having a baby shower, we hosted a Coming Out Brunch for the new baby and mother. Back then, some of us were still single and the rest of us were just starting our families. In all, we have had four Coming Out Brunches to celebrate our new babies and are gratified that our combined seven children are a close-knit unit in and of themselves. We are pleased to share our brunch menus with you in this chapter, as well as the breakfast menus we have cooked together on our yearly getaways.

Breakfast is one of our favorite events during our annual spring and fall trips together. Many times we will start the day with a devotional from one of our favorite books, then join together to prepare a spectacularly indulgent breakfast. Of course, we love to linger over coffee and discuss all things serious and light during this leisurely beginning to a promising day. We hope these menus will encourage our readers to establish a soothing breakfast tradition of their own.

Chicken Salad with Artichokes
Pecan Casserole
Susan's Apple Carrot Muffins
Taffy Apple Salad
Spiced Iced Tea

CHICKEN SALAD WITH ARTICHOKES

The Fab Five favorite salad. Great served on a bed of greens or as a sandwich on an onion roll.

4	chicken breast halves, cooked and cubed
1	14 oz. can artichoke hearts, drained and chopped
3/4	cup mayonnaise
3/4	cup chopped celery
6	green onions, chopped
1	cup chopped pecans, (toasted)
1/4	t. salt
1/8	t. garlic powder
1/8	t. pepper

Yield: 8 servings

Combine all ingredients, refrigerate until serving.

Note: This can also be prepared in a food processor.

PECAN CASSEROLE

Prepare the night before.

2 packages Little Sizzlers, cubed
1 loaf cinnamon raisin bread, cubed
6 eggs
1½ cup milk
1½ cup half and half
1 t. vanilla
¼ t. ground nutmeg
¼ t. ground cinnamon

Topping:
1 cup packed brown sugar
1 cup coarsely chopped pecans
½ cup butter, softened
2 T. maple syrup

Makes 8-10 servings

Grease a 9 × 13 pan. Place cubed bread in pan. Brown sausage, drain. Layer over cubed bread. Combine remaining ingredients; pour over bread and sausage. Store in refrigerator overnight.

Heat oven to 350°. Mix all topping ingredients together and crumble over surface of casserole. Bake uncovered 35 to 40 minutes.

SUSAN'S APPLE CARROT MUFFINS

Delicious and good for you, too!

2 cups flour
1¼ cup sugar
2 t. baking soda
2 t. cinnamon
2 t. salt
2 cups grated carrots
½ cup raisins
½ cup chopped pecans
½ cup coconut
1 cup Granny Smith apples, finely chopped
1 cup vegetable oil
3 eggs, lightly beaten
2 t. vanilla

Yield: 1½ dozen or 5-6 dozen mini

Preheat oven to 350°. Combine flour, sugar, baking soda, cinnamon and salt. Toss carrots, raisins, pecans, coconut and apples together. Add the mixture to the dry ingredients. Beat oil into eggs, add vanilla and combine with carrot mixture. It will be very thick. Pour into greased muffin tins and bake in preheated oven for 25 minutes for regular and 12-15 minutes for minis or until firm and lightly browned.

TAFFY APPLE SALAD

Mix and cook for 5 minutes until thick:

½   cup sugar
1   T. flour
2   T. Cider vinegar
1   egg, well beaten
Pineapple juice from a 9 oz. can of crushed pineapple, reserve crushed pineapple.

Yields: 8-10 servings

Refrigerate this overnight.

Next day mix the above mixture with 8 ounces of Cool Whip.

Then add:
4   cups diced apples
Reserved pineapple
1   cup salted roasted peanuts

SPICED ICED TEA

2   quarts water
3   cinnamon sticks
½   t. whole cloves
¼   t. ground nutmeg
4   family size tea bags
½   cup sugar
1   6 oz. can frozen orange juice concentrate
1   6 oz. can frozen lemonade concentrate

Yields: 2 quarts

Bring first 4 ingredients to a boil in a large Dutch oven. Remove from heat and add tea bags, cover and steep 5 minutes. Using a slotted spoon, remove and discard tea bags, cinnamon and cloves. Stir in sugar until dissolved; stir in orange juice and lemonade concentrates. Chill and serve over ice.

*To have a good friend is one of the highest delights of life;
to be a good friend is one of the noblest
and most difficult undertakings.*

Unknown

Sweet Onion and Cucumber Salad with Creamy Tomato Dressing
Strawberries Devonshire
Zucchini Frittata
Blueberry Buttermilk Coffee Cake
Champagne Cocktail

SWEET ONION AND CUCUMBER SALAD WITH CREAMY TOMATO DRESSING

Dressing:
¼ cup canned crushed tomato, undrained
¼ cup sour cream
¼ cup mayonnaise
¼ cup buttermilk
3 T. Dijon mustard
2 t. chopped fresh chives or green onion
2 t. chopped fresh basil (or ¾ t. dried)
2 t. chopped fresh parsley
2 t. chopped fresh cilantro
2 t. fresh lime juice
1½ t. minced shallot
½ t. minced garlic
8 cups mixed baby greens

1 small Maui onion (or other sweet white onion), sliced very thinly
1 cucumber, peeled and thinly sliced

Yield: 4-6 servings

Combine first 12 ingredients in food processor and blend just until smooth (do not overmix). Transfer to bowl. Season to taste with salt and pepper. Cover and refrigerate at least 4 hours. (Can be prepared 1 day ahead.) Combine greens, onion and cucumber in large bowl. Toss with enough dressing to coat.

STRAWBERRIES DEVONSHIRE

1   3 oz. package cream
     cheese (room
     temperature)
2   T. sugar
dash of salt
1   cup heavy cream,
     divided
fresh whole strawberries,
     stems on

Yield: 4 cups

In a small bowl combine cream cheese, sugar, salt and ½ cup of cream.

Beat until fluffy. Whip the remaining cream. Fold into cream cheese mixture.

Place in small serving bowl surrounded by berries.

ZUCCHINI FRITTATA

1½ cups chopped onion
2-3 T. butter (or olive oil)
½   lb. zucchini, peeled and
     shredded
12 eggs, beaten
2   T. fresh basil
     (or 2 t. dried)
2   t. salt
cracked pepper to taste
3   T. dried bread crumbs
2   cloves garlic, minced
2   tomatoes, peeled and
     sliced
1   cup grated parmesan
     cheese
1   cup grated cheddar
     cheese

Yield: 4-6 servings

Sauté onion in butter or oil, add zucchini and cook about 2 minutes. Slightly beat eggs and add basil, salt and pepper. Fold in onion, zucchini mixture, bread crumbs and garlic. Pour into buttered quiche dish, arrange tomatoes on top and sprinkle with cheddar and parmesan cheese. Bake at 350° for 20-25 minutes.

Ah, how good it feels! The hand of an old friend.

Henry Wadsworth Longfellow

BLUEBERRY BUTTERMILK COFFEE CAKE

Topping:
2/3 cup sugar
1/2 cup chopped pecans
2 T. butter, melted
1 1/2 t. ground cinnamon
1/2 t. ground nutmeg

Cake:
1 cup buttermilk
2 large eggs
2 t. vanilla extract
1 1/2 t. grated orange peel
2 cups flour
1 cup sugar
1 T. baking powder
1/4 t. ground nutmeg
1/2 cup chilled unsalted butter, cut into pieces
1 1/2 cups frozen unsweetened blueberries

Yield: 6-8 servings

Preheat oven to 350°. Butter 9 x 9 x 2 inch baking pan. Dust with flour.

For topping: Stir all ingredients in a small bowl to blend. Set aside.

For cake: Whisk buttermilk, eggs, vanilla and orange peel in small bowl until blended. Stir flour, sugar, baking powder and nutmeg in large bowl until blended. Using fingertips, rub butter into dry ingredients until mixture resembles coarse meal. Add buttermilk mixture and stir just until blended. Fold in berries.

Transfer batter to prepared pan. Sprinkle topping over top. Bake cake until tester inserted into center comes out clean, about 1 hour and 5 minutes. Cool cake completely in pan on rack.

CHAMPAGNE COCKTAILS

Fab Five love these cocktails

Chilled champagne glasses
Good-quality champagne
Sugar cubes
Angostura bitters

Soak the sugar cubes in the bitters. Drop one cube in each chilled champagne glass and fill with champagne.

Mexican Soufflé Appetizer
Avocado and Roasted Corn Guacamole
Migas by Debbie
Sangria Punch
Blueberry Salad

MEXICAN SOUFFLÉ APPETIZER

2	4 oz. cans whole green chilies, drained, rinsed and seeded
½	lb. sharp Cheddar Cheese, shredded
¾	cup dry breadcrumbs
3	eggs, beaten
1	t. parsley flakes
½	t. ground cumin
1	t. salt
1	t. oregano
½	cup light cream
½	cup milk

Yield: 12-15 servings

Grease 9 x 13 pan. Cover bottom of pan with chilies. Sprinkle cheese over the chilies. Spread bread crumbs over the cheese. Beat the eggs until light. Add rest of the ingredients to the eggs and beat again. Pour this mixture over the cheese. Bake at 375° for 40 minutes. Cool. Cut into squares.

There can be no friendship when there is no freedom.
Friendship loves the free air and will not be
fenced up in straight and narrow enclosures.

William Penn

AVOCADO AND ROASTED CORN GUACAMOLE WITH TOASTED CORN TORTILLAS

1 cup corn kernels, fresh or thawed frozen
¼ cup plus 3 T. corn oil
2 large avocados, cut into ½ inch dice
1 large tomato, cut into ¼ inch pieces
¼ cup chopped fresh cilantro
2 T. minced red onion
about 1 t. minced fresh or pickled jalapeño pepper
1 t. minced garlic
2 T. fresh lime juice
I t. cider vinegar
1½ t. coarse Kosher salt
¼ t. cumin
2 7 oz. package corn tortillas, quartered
table salt (for sprinkling)

Yield: 8 servings

Preheat the oven to 450°. On a baking sheet, toss the corn with 1 T. of the oil. Roast, tossing often, for 7 to 8 minutes, until golden. Let cool, then transfer to a medium bowl.

Fold in the avocado, tomato, cilantro, onion, jalapeño, and garlic. Stir in the lime juice, vinegar, coarse salt, cumin and 2 more T. of the corn oil. Cover and refrigerate for up to 6 hours.

Meanwhile, in a large bowl, toss the tortilla pieces with the remaining ¼ cup corn oil. Arrange half of the tortillas in a single layer on 2 large baking sheets. Bake for 5 to 6 minutes, or until crisp. Remove from the oven, transfer to paper towels and season with table salt. Repeat with the remaining tortillas and more salt. Serve warm with the cold guacamole.

"I never drink anything stronger than gin before breakfast.
W. C. Fields

MIGAS BY DEBBIE
Great with warmed flour tortillas

¼ cup oil
12 corn tortillas
½ cup coarsely chopped onion
6 eggs
1 cup coarsely chopped tomatoes
1 large jalapeño or 3 serrano chile peppers, finely chopped
½ t. black pepper
¾ t. salt
1 t. crushed and finely chopped garlic
1 cup shredded Monterey Jack or American cheese

Yield: 4-6 servings

In a large skillet, heat the oil to 350°. Cut or tear the tortillas into bite-size pieces. Sauté the tortillas until they are crisp. Add the onion and sauté for about 1 minute.

In a bowl, beat the eggs. Add the tomatoes, chile peppers, black pepper, salt and garlic and thoroughly beat them into the eggs.

Pour the egg mixture onto the tortillas. Cook the eggs 3 or 4 minutes, until they begin to set, stirring them in the process. Add the cheese and continue stirring until the eggs are completely set.

SANGRIA PUNCH

⅔ cup lemon juice
⅓ cup orange juice
¼ cup sugar
1 bottle (quart) dry red wine
fruit slices and lemon twist (optional for serving)

Yield: 6-8 servings
(½ cup each)

Strain juices, add sugar, stirring until dissolved. Just before serving mix juice mixture and wine in a pitcher. Add ice, serve with fruit slices or twist of lemon peel if desired.

11

BLUEBERRY SALAD

2   3 oz. package black cherry jello
2   cups boiling water
1   15 oz. can blueberries
1   8¼ oz. can crushed pineapple
1   8 oz. package cream cheese, softened
½   cup sugar
½   pint sour cream
1   t. vanilla
½   cup chopped pecans

Yield: 12-15 servings

Dissolve jello in boiling water; stir till dissolved. Drain blueberries and pineapple, reserve the liquid to measure 1 cup, add water if necessary. Add to the jello mixture. Stir in fruit. Pour into flat dish. Cover and refrigerate until firm. Combine cream cheese, sour cream, sugar and vanilla and whip until smooth. Spread on top of firm jello. Sprinkle pecans over creamed layer. Cover and refrigerate until ready to serve.

(This can be prepared well in advance; keeps well and can also be used as a dessert.)

The real friend is he or she who can share all our sorrow and double our joys.

B.C. Forbes

Herbed Brunch Casserole
Ham & Cheese Puffs
Sour Cream Coffee Cake
Kir Punch
Chocolate Mousse Cups

HERBED BRUNCH CASSEROLE
A Fab Five favorite

2½	cups herb-seasoned croutons
2	cups shredded sharp Cheddar Cheese (about 5½ ounces)
¼	lb. sliced mushrooms
2	lb. bulk sausage
6	eggs
2½	cups milk
1	can cream of mushroom soup
2¾	t. dry mustard

Yield: 12-15 servings

Preheat oven to 300°. Grease 9 x 13 inch baking dish. Arrange croutons in single layer on bottom of dish. Sprinkle cheese and mushrooms evenly over croutons. Cook sausage in large skillet, breaking into chunks, until browned, about 15 minutes. Add to baking dish. Beat eggs, milk, mushroom soup and mustard in medium bowl. Pour over sausage (can be prepared to this point and refrigerated overnight.) Bake until set, about 1½ hours. Serve hot.

Years and years of happiness only make us realize
how lucky we are to have friends who have shared
and made that happiness a reality.

Robert E. Frederick

13

HAM AND CHEESE PUFFS

2   sheets Pepperidge Farm frozen puff pastry, thawed
1/3   cup peach preserves
1/3   cup spicy prepared mustard
23   1 oz. slices of cooked ham
12   ¾ oz. slices Swiss cheese
2   egg yolks, beaten

Yield: 30 servings

Working with one portion at a time, roll each sheet of the puff pastry into a 18 × 9 inch rectangle on a lightly floured surface. Cut 15-3 inch squares from each portion of rolled dough. (Optional—cut 15–¾ inch rounds from each dough portion, these are used to top the squares).

Combine peach preserves and mustard; stir well. Spread about ½ t. on each square of dough, leaving a ¾ inch margin around the edges. Cut each ham square and each cheese square into 4–1½ inch squares. Layer a ham and cheese and another ham diagonally on one pastry square. Brush yolk over edges of square. Fold all corners to the middle; pinch edges to seal. Brush one side of a small round of dough with yolk; place on top of ham and cheese bundle, egg side down. Press slightly in center. Repeat procedure to use remaining ingredients. Place on ungreased baking sheets, and freeze at least 15 minutes. Bake at 425° for 15 to 17 minutes.

There is only one thing better than making a new friend, and that is keeping an old one.

Elmer G. Letterman

SOUR CREAM COFFEE CAKE

Easy & very good

1	cup margarine or butter, softened
3	cups sugar
2	eggs
1	t. vanilla
1	cup sour cream
2	cups flour
1	t. baking soda
½	t. salt
1	cup chopped pecans or walnuts
2	heaping T. cinnamon
4	heaping T. brown sugar

Yield: 12-15 servings

In a large bowl, cream together the first 5 ingredients. Mix the flour, baking soda and salt together and then add to the cream mixture. Spread half of this mixture into a 9 × 13 pan. In a separate bowl, mix together the nuts, cinnamon and sugar. Sprinkle the nut mixture over the spread batter. Spread the remaining batter over the nut mixture.

Bake at 350° for 50 to 60 minutes or until golden brown. (Test for doneness.)

KIR PUNCH

A great punch to serve for any celebration!

1 part white wine
1 part 7-up
Cream de Cassis to taste

Mix the 3 ingredients and refrigerate. Serve in a stemmed glass and garnish with a lemon twist. (Cream de Cassis is a Black Currant liqueur.)

As in the case of wines that improve with age, the oldest friendships ought to be the most delightful.

CHOCOLATE MOUSSE CUPS

These mousse cups bring back party memories.
They are delicious. The chocolate mousse is great served in
dessert goblets. Very easy and fancy.

1	cup heavy cream
2	large eggs
½	cup sugar
½	t. instant coffee granules
¼	cup water
2	T. Grand Marnier or Brandy
6	oz. semi-sweet chocolate

Milk chocolate cups and/or white chocolate cups

These can be store bought or made at home. Technique will follow if you want to make them at home.

(Mousse makes enough for approximately 48 cups or so)

Whip the cream until thick, set aside. Heat the sugar and water in a saucepan until sugar is dissolved and the mixture comes to a boil. Stir in the chocolate. With an electric mixer, process the eggs and coffee for several seconds. With the mixer running, pour in the chocolate syrup slowly and process until smooth. Add the Grand Marnier or Brandy, if desired. Spoon the cream into the bowl and mix slightly until just blended.

Pour into several small bowls so that in order to pipe the mousse into the chocolate cups the process will be easier and the mousse will not thin out. (This mousse will be very thin at first but thickens after several hours in the refrigerator.)

(Continued on Next Page)

CHOCOLATE CUPS:

Milk chocolate (better quality chocolate will work best)
White chocolate
Candy molds (many shapes will work, we use ones shaped like peanut butter cups – the small ones)
(Chocolate cups are time consuming. Do before hand and refrigerate.)

Yield: 48 individual cups

Melt the chocolate in a double boiler. Lightly spray the candy molds with non-stick spray. Using a cooking paint brush line the candy mold with chocolate. Line thick enough to stay solid. After filling a tray put in it in the freezer a few minutes to harden chocolate. Pop cups out of tray holding tray close to the counter top to avoid many breaking.

Assembly of the mousse cups:

Fill pastry bag with mousse and pipe into individual chocolate cups. Refrigerate until serving.

Optional: When strawberries are in season, garnish with ¼ piece of strawberry.

*If you have an old friend you haven't called in a while,
why not pick up the telephone today?
The call won't cost much. And besides,
the king has an unlisted number.*

Hot Artichoke Cheese Squares
Poppy Seed Bread
Southern Breakfast Casserole
Brandy Slush
Red Berry Mousse

HOT ARTICHOKE-CHEESE SQUARES

2	T. oil
1/3	cup finely chopped onion
1	clove garlic, mashed
4	eggs
1	14 oz. can artichoke hearts, drained
1/2	cup dry bread crumbs
1/2	lb. Swiss or sharp cheddar cheese, shredded
2	T. minced parsley
1/2	t. salt
1/2	t. pepper
1/4	t. oregano
1/8	t. Tabasco sauce

Yield: 8-12 servings

Grease a baking dish approximately 7 x 11. Preheat oven to 325°. In skillet, heat oil and sauté onion and garlic until limp but not brown. Beat eggs to froth in mixing bowl, chop artichokes in small pieces and add to bowl. Stir in onion, bread crumbs, cheese, parsley and seasonings. Turn mixture into baking pan and bake for 25 to 30 minutes until set when lightly touched.

Let cool a bit, cut into 1 1/2 inch squares. If you make ahead, refrigerate, then reheat in a 325° oven for 10 minutes.

Makes 36 squares.

POPPY SEED BREAD

3 cups flour
2½ cups sugar
3 eggs
1½ t. salt
1½ cups oil
1½ t. baking powder
1½ cups milk
1½ t. vanilla
1½ t. almond flavoring
1½ t butter flavoring
1½ T. poppy seeds

Yield: 12-15 servings

Mix all ingredients together. Beat 2 minutes. Bake at 350° for 1 hour and 15 minutes in greased and floured pans. Makes two large loaves.

Glaze:
½ cup orange juice
½ cup sugar
½ t. each vanilla, almond and butter flavoring
Mix and pour immediately over bread.

SOUTHERN BREAKFAST CASSEROLE

Good hearty casserole – men love it!

4-8 English muffins, halved
1 lb. sausage cooked and drained
2 cups cheese
4 eggs
1 can mushroom soup
2 cups milk
½ cup water

Yield: 12 servings

Line 9 × 13 casserole dish with halved English muffins. Add sausage. Mix all other ingredients together and one cup of the cheese and pour over sausage. Put remaining cup of cheese over the sausage. Bake 325° for 1 hour and 15 minutes.

BRANDY SLUSH

7 cups water
1½ cups sugar
1 12 oz. frozen lemonade concentrate
1 12 oz. frozen orange juice
1½ cups brandy
7-Up

Yields 23-8 oz. servings

Boil water and sugar. Cool. Add lemonade, orange juice, and brandy. Freeze 24 hours or longer. To serve, fill glass half full with slush mixture. Fill with 7-Up and stir.

19

RED BERRY MOUSSE

1   envelope unflavored
    gelatin
2   T. cold water
Juice of 1 lemon
Grated zest of 1 lemon
1   pint strawberries, rinsed,
    drained, hulled and
    quartered
1   pint raspberries, rinsed
    and drained
2   T. crème de cassis
2   eggs yolks
½   cup sugar
2   cups whipping cream
¼   t. cinnamon
Fresh mint sprigs, for garnish

Yield: 6 servings

Combine the gelatin and water in a small saucepan, and set aside to soak for 5 minutes.

Stir the lemon juice into the softened gelatin. Then add the zest, raspberries (reserving a few for garnish), strawberries and Cassis. Bring gently to a boil, stirring frequently, and then set aside to cool to room temperature.

Combine the egg yolks and sugar in a small bowl, and beat until pale yellow. Transfer the mixture to a double boiler and cook over simmering water, whisking, until hot and slightly thickened, 10 to 15 minutes. Set aside to cool.

Fold the berry mixture thoroughly into the cooled custard.

Whip the cream and cinnamon with an electric mixer until it forms soft peaks and gently fold it into the mixture. Scoop the mousse into a glass bowl or large individual wine goblets and refrigerate until set.

Garnish with the reserved raspberries and sprig of mint and serve.

(Cream de Cassis is a black Currant Liqueur.)

Sausage Roll Puffs
Sparkling Strawberry Mimosa
Cheesy Hot Artichoke Dip
Figs with Ricotta, Honey and Walnuts

SAUSAGE ROLL PUFFS

1 pound puff pastry
1 pound well-seasoned
   sausage meat

Yield: 90 puffs

Roll the puff pastry into a rectangle 15½ × 9 inches and cut the rectangle into three strips, each 3 inches wide. Divide the sausage meat into thirds and roll each into a "snake" the length of the pastry. Place each roll of sausage along one edge of a pastry strip. Roll the pastry around the sausage and wet the edges with ice water and press to seal tightly. Chill the rolls for at least an hour. Preheat the oven to 400°.

Cut the sausage rolls into ½ inch slices and put them on parchment covered baking sheets. Bake until the pastry is puffed and golden brown tipping the baking dish slightly to allow grease to drain, about 12 minutes. Serve warm or reheat immediately before serving

Note the sausage rolls can be sliced and frozen before they are cooked. To bake, preheat the oven to 400° and cook the frozen puff as above.

SPARKLING STRAWBERRY MIMOSA

2½ cups orange juice, chilled
1 10 oz. package frozen strawberries, partially thawed
1 26.4 oz. bottle dry champagne, chilled
whole strawberries, optional

Yield: 8 cups

Combine orange juice and partially thawed strawberries in container of electric blender. Process until puréed. Pour into pitcher. Add champagne. Stir gently. Garnish each serving with whole strawberry, if desired. Serve immediately.

CHEESY HOT ARTICHOKE DIP

Always a party favorite

1 4 oz. jar pimientos diced
1 14 oz. can artichoke hearts, drained and chopped
1½ cups mayonnaise
1 7 oz. can green chiles, drained and diced
4 oz. Monterey jack cheese, (shredded)
½ cup grated Parmesan cheese
additional grated Parmesan cheese
corn chips or tortilla chips
(Variation: add 2-6 oz. package of frozen crabmeat)

Yield: 12-15 serving

Preheat oven to 325°. Drain pimientos and reserve 2 t. of pimientos for garnish. In medium bowl, mix pimientos, artichokes, mayonnaise, green chiles, Monterey jack cheese and ½ cup Parmesan cheese. Spread mixture into a shallow 1½ quart baking dish. Sprinkle with additional Parmesan cheese and 2 t. of pimientos. (Can be made ahead. Cover and refrigerate.) Bake uncovered 30 minutes until bubbly. Serve with corn chips or tortilla chips.

FIGS WITH RICOTTA, HONEY AND WALNUTS

15	fresh figs, trimmed
½	cup whole-milk ricotta cheese
⅓	cup honey
⅓	cup chopped walnuts

Yield: 5 servings

Cut each fig into 4 wedges, cutting to, but not through, base of fig. Spread wedges slightly apart; place 3 figs on each of 5 dessert plates. Spoon about 1½ t. cheese into each fig, and spoon about 1 T. honey evenly around each serving of figs. Sprinkle each serving of figs with about 1 T. walnuts. (Note: Dried figs may be substituted for fresh figs.)

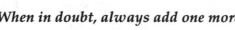

When in doubt, always add one more!

Fab Five

Tomato with Feta Cheese and Capers

Basil and Tomato Frittata

Brown Sugar Bacon

Bubble Bread

Planter's Punch

This whole menu is fabulous and fairly easy.

TOMATO WITH FETA CHEESE AND CAPERS

2	medium tomatoes
8	T. Feta cheese
4	t. capers

Yield: 4 servings

Half the tomatoes and sprinkle each half with 2 T. Feta cheese and 1 t. capers.

BASIL AND TOMATO FRITTATA

10	eggs
½	cup milk
¾	cup grated cheddar cheese
2	tomatoes, chopped
⅓	cup fresh basil, chopped

Salt and pepper to taste

Yield: 4-5 servings

Beat eggs and add other ingredients. Pour into a casserole dish sprayed with non-stick vegetable spray. Bake at 350° for 45 minutes or until done.

BROWN SUGAR BACON

8   slices of bacon
¾   cup brown sugar

Yield: 4 servings

Use any bacon you desire. Roll in brown sugar and place on a Jelly roll pan. Bake at 400° degrees until done. Remove from pan; drain on baking racks.

(Do not drain on paper towels.)

BUBBLE BREAD

1   loaf French bread
⅓   cup Parmesan cheese
⅓   cup Hellman's mayonnaise

Yield: 8 servings

Mix cheese and mayonnaise. Slice loaf in 1 inch width slices. Spread mixture on bread. Bake at 400° until bread starts to bubble.

PLANTER'S PUNCH

3   T. fresh lime juice
3   T. fresh lemon juice
1   T. superfine sugar
½   t. grenadine
¾   cup fresh orange juice
¾   cup pineapple juice
½   cup club soda
½   cup dark rum
½   cup light rum
16   ice cubes
Orange slices and cherries for garnish

Yield: 6-8 servings

Combine all ingredients except garnish in a large pitcher and stir well. Pour into tumblers with ice and garnish with orange slices and cherries.

Increase the amount of club soda if you prefer a punch without rum.

Cheese and Pesto Spread
Petite Cream Puffs
Sausage Stuffed Mushrooms
Roasted Red Bell Pepper Appetizer
Strawberry Lemonade Mimosa

CHEESE AND PESTO SPREAD

*This is tasty and has a beautiful
presentation when unmoled.*

1   8 oz. package cream cheese
1   4½ oz. package Brie cheese
1   cup firmly packed fresh basil leaves
½   cup firmly packed parsley sprigs
½   cup grated Parmesan cheese
¼   cup pine nuts, walnuts, or almonds
2   cloves garlic, quartered
¼   cup olive oil or cooking oil
½   cup whipping cream
Crackers or sliced French bread

Yield: 24 servings

Soften cream cheese and Brie cheese. For pesto, in a blender combine basil, parsley, Parmesan cheese, nuts, garlic and two tbsp. oil. Cover; blend with on-off turns till a paste forms. Gradually add remaining oil, blending on low speed till smooth.

Beat cream cheese and Brie together till nearly smooth. Beat whipping cream till soft peaks form. Fold whipped cream into cheese mixture.

Line a 3½ or 4-cup mold with plastic wrap. Spread one-fourth of cheese mixture into mold. Top with one-third of pesto. Repeat layers twice. Top with cheese mixture. Chill 6-24 hours.

To serve, unmold on plate. Remove plastic wrap. Garnish with fresh basil, if desired. Serve w/crackers or French bread.

PETITE CREAM PUFFS

These always cause a rave.

Cream Puff filling:
¾   cup flour
1   cup sugar
dash of salt
3   cups milk
6   egg yolks
1   t. vanilla

Combine flour, sugar and salt. Mix together milk and egg yolks, strain and add slowly to dry mixture. Mix well, avoiding lumps. Cook over medium heat until thick. Take filling off heat and add vanilla. Cool.

CRÈME PUFFS

½   cup water
¼   cup butter or margarine
½   cup flour
2   eggs
powdered sugar

Yield: 12-15 small puffs

Heat oven to 400°. Heat water and butter to rolling boil in a saucepan. Stir in flour. Stir vigorously over low heat until mixture forms a ball, about 1 minute; remove from heat. Beat in eggs, all at once; continue beating until smooth. Drop a scant teaspoon full of dough about 2 inches apart onto un-greased cookie sheet.

Bake until puffed and golden, 20 to 25 minutes. Cool away from draft. Cut off tops, pull out any filaments of soft dough. Fill puffs with cream filling. Replace tops; dust with powdered sugar. Refrigerate until serving time.

Old friends are the great blessing of one's later years.
They have a memory of the same events
and have the same mode of thinking.

SAUSAGE-STUFFED MUSHROOMS

2   Italian sweet sausages, about 1/3 lb.
1/4   t. Fennel seeds
Pinch of red pepper flakes (optional)
1/4   cup finely minced yellow onion
1   garlic clove, peeled and minced
Olive oil, as necessary
1/4   cup parsley, chopped
1/4   cup black olives, chopped
1/3   cup thick Béchamel sauce (See recipe on next page)
Salt and freshly ground black pepper, to taste
12   large white mushrooms
Parmesan cheese to taste

Yield: 3-4 servings

Remove sausage meat from casings and crumble into a small skillet. Sauté gently, stirring often, until meat is thoroughly done. Season with fennel seeds and, if desired, red pepper flakes. With a slotted spoon, remove sausage to a bowl, leaving the rendered fat in the skillet.

Sauté onion and garlic in the rendered fat adding a little olive oil if necessary, until tender and golden, about 25 minutes. Stir in chopped parsley and add to reserved sausage meat.

Stir olives and béchamel into the sausage mixture; combining thoroughly. Taste the mixture and season with salt and pepper if necessary.

Pull the stems off the mushrooms and save for another use. Wipe mushroom caps with a damp cloth and season lightly with salt and pepper.

Fill each cap generously with the stuffing. Arrange caps in a lightly oiled baking dish. Sprinkle the tops with Parmesan cheese to taste.

Bake at 450° for about 15 minutes or until bubbling and well browned. Let settle for 5 minutes before serving.

(Continued on Next Page)

BÉCHAMEL SAUCE

4   T. sweet butter
6   T. unbleached all-purpose
     flour
2   cups milk
Salt, freshly ground black
     pepper and freshly grated
     nutmeg, to taste

Yield: 2 cups thick sauce

Melt butter in a heavy saucepan. Sprinkle in the flour and cook gently, stirring almost constantly for 5 minutes. Do not let the flour and butter brown at all.

Meanwhile, bring the milk to a boil. When milk reaches a boil, remove butter and flour mixture from heat and pour in the boiling milk all at once. As the mixture boils and bubbles, beat it vigorously with a wire whisk.

When the bubbling stops, return the pan to medium heat and bring the béchamel to a boil, stirring constantly for 5 minutes. Season to taste with salt, pepper and nutmeg. Use at once or scrape into a bowl, cover and refrigerate until needed.

Note: For 2 cups medium sauce; use 3 tablespoons butter and 4 tablespoons all-purpose flour with the same amount of milk.

ROASTED RED
BELL PEPPER APPETIZER

Very tasty and easy

7   oz. roasted red bell
     peppers; drained and diced
1   T. purple onion, diced
1   t. garlic, diced
½   t. black pepper
1   T. basil (fresh when
     possible)
1   T. olive oil
Carr's Crackers
Mozzarella cheese, sliced
     thinly
Roma tomatoes, sliced thinly

Yield: 12 appetizer servings

Combine first five ingredients in a small bowl. Drizzle olive oil over mixture immediately before serving. Best served at room temperature.

Stack a Carr's Cracker, sliced mozzarella cheese, sliced Roma tomato, and a dollop of red bell pepper mixture.

STRAWBERRY LEMONADE MIMOSA

Very nice. Add a sprig of mint to top it off!

1   10 oz can of Strawberry
      Daiquiri Bacardi Mixer
2   cups Minute Maid
      Premium Pink Lemonade
1   bottle champagne or
      sparkling apple cider

Yield: 8 servings

Combine the strawberry Daiquiri Mixer and the Minute Maid pink lemonade until dissolved.

In each champagne glass, fill halfway with the strawberry-lemonade mixture. Fill to top with champagne or cider; stir and serve.

Asparagus Roll-ups
Zesty Crab and Artichoke Dip
Southwestern Cheesecake
Chocolate-Lemon Creams

ASPARAGUS ROLL-UPS

14 thin slices white bread, crusts trimmed
8 slices bacon, cooked crisp, drained, and crumbled
8 oz. cream cheese, room temperature
Finely grated zest of 1 lemon
28 asparagus spears, cooked crisp-tender
Melted unsalted butter

Yield: 28 hors d'oerves

Flatten the bread slices with a rolling pin. Combine the bacon, cream cheese, and lemon zest. Spread an even layer of the cream cheese mixture on each flattened bread slice.

Place 2 asparagus spears, with the tips facing in opposite directions, on one edge of each bread slice. Roll up each slice like a jellyroll. Cut each roll in half and place seam side down on a lightly greased cookie sheet.*

Preheat broiler. Brush the tops and sides of the roll-ups with melted butter. Broil 6 inches from the heat until lightly browned and toasted. Serve immediately.

*The roll-ups can be prepared up to this point 3 hours in advance. Store covered in the refrigerator.

ZESTY
CRAB-AND-ARTICHOKE DIP

This dip can be prepared ahead of time to cut down on last-minute preparation time.
Assemble the ingredients and spoon them into the baking dish. Cover the dish and refrigerate for up to 4 hours.

1   large green pepper, chopped
2   14 oz. cans artichoke hearts, drained and finely chopped
1   cup mayonnaise
1   cup plain yogurt
2/3   cup grated Parmesan cheese
½   cup thinly sliced scallions
½   cup bottled roasted sweet red peppers, drained and chopped
5   t. lemon juice
4   t. Worcestershire sauce
1   T. seeded and finely chopped pickled jalapeño peppers (wear plastic gloves when handling)
¼   t. celery seeds
1   lb. lump crabmeat, picked over and flaked
*Can use 2 cans (6 oz.) crabmeat, drained and flaked
¼   cup sliced almonds (optional)

Yield: 22 servings (¼ cup each). If halving the recipe, bake it in an 8-inch round cake pan for about 25 minutes.

Coat a small skillet with nonstick spray. Add the green peppers. Cook and stir over medium heat for 3 minutes, or until tender; let cool at room temperature. Preheat oven to 375°. Coat an 8 x 8 baking pan with nonstick spray. In a large bowl, combine the cooked peppers, artichoke hearts, mayonnaise, yogurt, Parmesan cheese, scallions, red peppers, lemon juice, Worcestershire sauce, jalapeño peppers and celery seeds. Gently stir in the crabmeat. Spoon into the prepared baking pan. Sprinkle with the almonds, if desired. Bake for 30 to 35 minutes, or until golden brown and bubbly.

(To serve, bake the dip for 40 to 45 minutes if refrigerated.)

SOUTHWESTERN CHEESECAKE

Looks great on your party table!

1½ cups tortilla chips, finely crushed
5 T. unsalted butter, melted.
2 (8 oz.) pkgs cream cheese, softened
2 eggs
1 lb. ground beef
1 Package of taco seasoning
2 cups shredded cheddar cheese
1 med. can green chilies, chopped and drained
1 can refried beans
⅓ cup each of red and yellow pepper, chopped
1 small can sliced black olives
Tortilla chips

Yield: 24 servings

Crust:
Heat oven to 325°. Stir tortilla chips into melted butter. Press onto bottom of 9-inch springform pan and bake 15 minutes.

Filling:
With electric mixer, mix softened cream cheese, eggs, and pkg. of taco seasoning. Add cheese and green chilies

Brown ground beef. Drain, mix in can of refried beans. Spread cream cheese mixture over baked crust. Spread beef mixture over cream cheese layer. Place pan back in oven for 30 minutes at 325°.

Garnish with red and yellow peppers, black olives, and tortilla chips. Refrigerate-and serve *cold*.

When you are young and without success,
you have only a few friends.
Then, later on, when you are rich and famous,
you still have a few . . . if you are lucky.

Pablo Picasso

CHOCOLATE-LEMON CREAMS
Very good bite size dessert

2   8 oz. packages cream cheese, softened
2   T. grated lemon rind
3   T. fresh lemon Juice
1   t. lemon extract
1   cup sifted powdered sugar
12 2 oz. chocolate candy coating squares
2   2 oz. vanilla candy coating squares (optional)

Yield: 6 dozen

Beat first 5 ingredients at medium speed with an electric mixer until smooth: cover. Freeze 2 hours.

Shape cream cheese mixture into 1 inch balls, and place on a wax paper lined baking sheet: cover and freeze 1 hour. Let stand at room temperature 10 minutes.

Microwave chocolate candy coating in a 1-quart microwave-safe bowl at high 1½ minutes, stirring twice.

Dip balls into coating: place on wax paper. Let stand until firm.

Place vanilla coating in a ziplock plastic bag. Seal and submerge coating in warm water until melted. Snip a hole in 1 corner of bag, and drizzle coating over chocolates, if desired.

Note: A food processor may be used for the first step.

FAB FIVE FOOTNOTES

For party sandwiches cut your bread into shapes with cookie cutters for different occasions.

For a twist, add a pinch of cinnamon and ground cloves to your ground coffee.

For a new twist to your whipped cream, add a dash of cinnamon.

Before you whip your cream, put your bowl and beaters in the freezer until chilled.

Egg whites will have more volume if they are at room temperature before beating.

To prevent drying, take bacon out of package and wrap bacon in foil.

Store fresh asparagus upright in about 1 inch of water in refrigerator until needed.

When a recipe calls for eggs to be at room temperature, immerse refrigerated eggs, still in their shell, in warm water for a few minutes.

Bacon trick: Coat bacon with flour to keep from curling.

Champagne is best if chilled only 24 hours before serving.

NOTES

COMFORT FOODS

In the childhood memories of every good cook,
there is a large kitchen, a warm stove,
a simmering pot and a mom.

Barbara Costikyan

COMFORT FOODS

Setting the table is a basic part of all of our meals. We can make a table out of almost anything, the tailgate of a Suburban, a blanket, an airplane tray, a porch, you name it, we will accept the challenge of making it into a table with flowers, coordinating napkins, and dinnerware suitable for a splendid repast. We even took our dining accessories with us down a steep hill to a bridge where we set up with table, candles, music, and food to watch a spectacular sunset, moon rise, and the stars come out one by one. We danced and sang to the best of country rhythms in Jayton, Texas. For us, the greatest pleasure in cooking is creating a delicious meal that stimulates conversation and good feelings. We believe the table setting is always a vital ingredient in the pleasure of any meaningful meal.

This chapter includes our collection of cozy-down soups, stews, and casseroles. They aren't fancy, but they are mighty fine. All they need is the finest ingredients and a beautifully displayed table to bring out the very best in your guests. So set a lovely table and see how memorable a nurturing bowl of soup can be!

Fried Asparagus Parmesan

Gourmet Chicken Casserole

Your Classic Chess Pie

FRIED ASPARAGUS PARMESAN

2½ pounds fresh asparagus
1½ cups bread crumbs,
     toasted
1½ cups parmesan cheese,
     grated
4   eggs, lightly beaten
½   t. salt
pepper to taste
½   t. ground nutmeg
3-6 T. butter

Yield: 4 to 6 servings

Parboil asparagus. Place bread crumbs in shallow dish. Place parmesan cheese in another shallow dish. In a shallow bowl, combine eggs, salt, pepper and nutmeg. Dip stalk of asparagus in egg mixture, roll in cheese, dip in egg again and roll in bread crumbs. Coat remaining stalks in same manner. Chill for 30 minutes. In large skillet, sauté asparagus in butter until golden brown.

GOURMET CHICKEN CASSEROLE

This is a Fab Five favorite. It will be yours too.

2	cups diced boiled chicken
¼	cup mayonnaise
1	cup cooked rice
½	t. salt
4	oz. can mushrooms
1	cup diced celery
1	T. lemon juice
1	T. chopped onion
½	cup shredded almonds
1	can cream of chicken soup
1	cup crushed corn flakes
2	T. butter, melted

Yield: 6-8 servings

Combine all ingredients except corn flakes and butter and place in buttered 9 x 13 casserole. Mix corn flakes and butter together and place on top of casserole. Bake 30-40 minutes at 350°.

YOUR CLASSIC CHESS PIE

1	refrigerated piecrust
2	cups sugar
2	T. cornmeal
1	T. flour
¼	t. salt
½	cup butter, melted
¼	cup milk
1	T. white vinegar
½	t. vanilla extract
4	large eggs, lightly beaten

Yield: 1 (9 inch) pie

Bake pie crust according to directions on box. Cool.

Stir together sugar and next 7 ingredients until blended. Add eggs, stirring well. Pour into piecrust. Bake at 350° for 50 to 55 minutes, shielding edges with aluminum foil after 10 minutes to prevent excessive browning. Cool completely on a wire rack.

"I come from a home where gravy is a beverage."

Erma Bombeck

Fabulous Five Chili
Green Chile Cornbread
Chocolate Chip Pound Cake

FABULOUS FIVE CHILI

Time consuming but worth it! Not just your average chili.

¼	cup olive oil
1	onion, coarsely chopped
1	pound sweet Italian sausage meat, removed from casings
1	T. ground black pepper
1	can, 12 oz. tomato paste
1	can, 12 oz. tomato sauce
1½	T. minced garlic
1	T. ground cumin
2	oz. chili powder
¼	cup Dijon-style mustard
2	T. salt
2	T. dried basil
2	T. dried oregano
3	cans, 12 oz. Italian plum tomatoes, drained
¼	cup Burgundy wine
2	T. lemon juice
¼	cup chopped Italian parsley
2	cans, 16 oz. each, dark red kidney beans, drained
2	cans, 5½ oz. each, pitted black olives, drained

Yield: 8-10 servings

Heat olive oil in a very large pot. Add onions and cook over low heat, covered, until tender, about 10 minutes. Crumble sausage meat and cook over medium-high heat, stirring often, until meat is browned. Drain. Over low heat, stir in black pepper, tomato paste, tomato sauce, garlic, cumin, chili powder, mustard, salt, basil and oregano. Add drained tomatoes, Burgundy wine, lemon juice, parsley and drained kidney beans. Stir well and simmer, uncovered, for another 15 minutes.

Taste for additional seasonings. Add black olives and simmer for another 5 minutes and serve immediately.

May add additional toppings of sour cream, shredded cheese, or fritos.

41

GREEN CHILE CORNBREAD

2	eggs
1	8 oz. can cream style corn
1	cup sour cream
1	3 oz. can jalapeños, chopped or 2 oz. mild green chilies
1	cup grated cheddar cheese
1	cup yellow cornmeal
1	t. baking soda
6	T. butter

Yield: 8 servings

Preheat oven to 400°. In a bowl, beat eggs lightly with wire whisk. Add corn, sour cream, peppers, cheese, cornmeal and soda. Mix all ingredients. Add 3 T. melted butter. In a 9 x 9 pan or 10" cast iron skillet, melt 3 T. butter. While pan is still hot, add mixture and bake 20-25 minutes.

CHOCOLATE CHIP POUND CAKE

¾	cup sugar
2	large eggs
2	t. vanilla extract
10	T. unsalted butter, melted (1 ¼ sticks)
¼	cup milk
2	cups all purpose flour
1	t. baking powder
½	cup semisweet chocolate chips

Yield: 6-8 slices

Preheat oven to 325°. Butter and flour 9 x 5 x 3 inch loaf pan. Beat sugar, eggs and vanilla in large bowl until thick and blended. Add butter and beat until well blended. Beat in milk. Mix flour and baking powder in medium bowl. Add dry ingredients to butter mixture and stir just until blended. Mix in chocolate chips.

Spoon batter into prepared pan. Bake until cake is light golden and tester inserted into center of cake comes out clean, about 1 hour. Transfer pan to rack and cool 10 minutes. Turn out cake onto rack and cool completely.

Chicken Gumbo

Jan's Whole-Wheat Cornbread

Bourbon Pie

CHICKEN GUMBO

The Jones family loves this gumbo.

5 lbs. stewing chicken
flour for dredging
¼ cup rendered bacon fat
9 cups boiling water
2 cups chopped, seeded, peeled tomatoes
½ cup fresh corn kernels, cut from 1 small ear
1 cup sliced okra
1 large green pepper
½ t. salt
¼ cup diced onion
¼ cup raw unprocessed rice

Yield: 16 servings

Cut the chicken into pieces, and dredge each piece in flour. Brown the chicken pieces in the bacon fat, then pour in 4 cups of boiling water. Simmer the chicken, uncovered, until the meat falls from the bones. Drain the broth. Bone, skin and chop the meat. Reserve the meat and broth.

In a soup kettle place the tomatoes, okra, corn, pepper, salt, onion and rice, and the remaining 5 cups of water. Simmer uncovered until the vegetables and rice are tender, about 25 minutes. Combine this with the chicken and broth, correct the seasoning. Reheat the soup.

Serve over rice with cornbread or hard bread.

JAN'S WHOLE-WHEAT CORNBREAD

Using whole grains gives this cornbread a different taste.
Try it—you will love it.

½ cup whole-wheat flour
1 cup whole-grain yellow cornmeal
1 t. salt
1 t. baking powder
½ t. baking soda
2 eggs
1 cup (approx.) buttermilk
Oil

Yield: approximately 12 sticks

Preheat oven to 450° degrees. Mix together dry ingredients. Pour a small amount of oil in bottom of each muffin cup or cornbread stick pan. Heat in oven for 5 minutes. While heating pan, add 2 eggs and enough buttermilk (approx. 1 cup) to make a thick but pourable mixture. Beat well with spoon. Pour or dip cornbread batter into heated pan. Bake for 15-20 minutes to desired doneness. Immediately turn sticks or muffins over to prevent sweating and sticking.

BOURBON PIE

1 unbaked pie shell
½ cup flour
1 cup sugar
1 stick soft butter
2 eggs, slightly beaten
1 T. bourbon (or vanilla)
1 cup chocolate chips
1 cup chopped walnuts or pecans

Yield: 6-8 servings

Mix with spoon, flour, sugar and butter. Add eggs, and bourbon. Stir in chips and nuts and pour into unbaked shell. Bake at 375° for 30 minutes.

Granddad's Cornbread Salad

Chicken Enchilada Soup

Easiest Key Lime Pie

GRANDDAD'S CORNBREAD SALAD

Best salad during tomato season

1   recipe of cornbread
     (best made night before)

Chop:

3   large tomatoes, chopped
     (will stir in last)
2   green bell peppers,
     chopped
½   to 1 white onion, chopped
1   cup mayonnaise
     (the real stuff)
1   T. mustard
salt and pepper (to taste)

Yield: 8-10 servings

Crumble cornbread and mix all other ingredients together. Remember to add the tomatoes last just before serving.

"Only the pure of heart can make a good soup."

Ludwig Van Beethoven

Chicken Enchilada Soup

Great on a cold winter's night

4   chicken breasts,
     cooked and cubed
2   cloves garlic, minced
1   large onion, chopped
¼   cup butter
¼ to ½ cup flour
4   cans chicken broth
1   (4 oz.) can green chilies,
     chopped
1   (8 oz.) sour cream
1   (8 oz.) package shredded
     Velveeta cheese
8   corn tortillas cut in small
     pieces
salt and pepper (to taste)

Yield: 6-8 servings

In large pan melt butter, add onions and garlic. Sauté until transparent. Add flour to make a paste. Cook for one minute. Add 3 cans of broth and green chilies. Cook and stir until thickened (at this point see if you need the fourth can of broth). Stir in chicken, tortillas and shredded cheese. Cook over low heat until cheese is melted and tortillas softened. Stir in sour cream. Warm through but DO NOT BOIL. Salt and pepper to taste. Serve in soup bowls.

Laughing with Friends

*Few sounds on earth can compare with
the reverberations of friends laughing together.
Heartly laughter is oil in the engine of friendship:
With laughter, things run smoothly;
without it, the gears have a tendency to grind.*

EASIEST KEY LIME PIE

3   eggs, separated
1   (14 oz.) can Eagle brand sweetened condensed milk
½   cup ReaLime lime juice concentrate
Several drops green food coloring (optional)
1   (9 inch) unbaked piecrust
½   t. cream of tartar
⅓   cup sugar

Yield: 8 servings

Preheat oven to 325°. With mixer, beat egg yolks in medium-sized bowl; gradually beat in Eagle brand and ReaLime. Stir in food coloring if desired. Pour into piecrust. Bake 30 minutes.

Meanwhile, for meringue, with clean beaters, beat egg whites with cream of tartar to soft peaks. Gradually beat in sugar, 1 tablespoon at a time. Beat 4 minutes longer or until stiff, glossy peaks form and sugar is dissolved.

Remove pie from oven. Increase temperature to 350°. Immediately spread meringue over hot pie, carefully sealing to edge of crust. Bake 15 minutes. Cool 1 hour. Chill at least 3 hours. Store leftovers covered in refrigerator.

Acquaintances ask about our outward life;
friends ask about our inner life.

Marie von Ebner-Eschenbach

Old Fashioned Chicken and Rice
Frozen Fruit Salad
Spinach and Cheese Casserole
Pumpkin Cheesecake Bars

OLD FASHIONED CHICKEN AND RICE

6	boneless chicken breasts
7	pieces of raw bacon
2	cups of brown rice
1	can cream of chicken soup
1	can cream of mushroom soup
1	can cream of celery soup
¼	cup of water

salt and pepper (to taste)
seasoning salt (to taste)

Yield: 6 servings

Line 9 x 13 casserole baking dish with raw bacon. Add as a layer, the uncooked brown rice. Layer pieces of chicken on top. Next add salt, pepper and seasoning salt. Mix all three soups together and spoon over the chicken. Add the water. Cook uncovered for 1 hour at 350°.

Can be made without the bacon but add ½ cup more water.

"Of soup and love, the first is best."

Spanish Proverb

FROZEN FRUIT SALAD

The family will love this salad—especially the kids.

1	8 oz. pkg. cream cheese
¾	cup sugar
1	8 oz. can crushed pineapple, drained
1	10 oz. pkg. frozen strawberries
3	bananas, diced
1	cup chopped pecans if desired
1	9 oz. carton Cool Whip

Yield: 8 servings

Mix all ingredients and freeze in 8 × 8 pan or individual dessert cups. Thaw 10 minutes or more before serving.

SPINACH AND CHEESE CASSEROLE

1	cup flour
1	t. salt
1	t. baking powder
2	beaten eggs
1	cup milk
1	stick of margarine, melted
1	package frozen chopped spinach, thawed, drained, uncooked
1	16 oz. package sharp cheddar cheese

Yield: 12-15 servings

Mix together the flour, salt and baking powder. In a separate bowl, mix the slightly beaten eggs, milk and margarine. Combine the wet ingredients to the dry ingredients and then add the spinach and cheddar cheese.

Put all of this in a 9 × 13 greased casserole pan. Bake at 350° for 30 minutes.

True friends are the ones who really know you but love you anyway.

Edna Buchanan

PUMPKIN CHEESECAKE BARS

1	16 oz. package pound cake mix
3	eggs
2	T. butter, melted
4	t. pumpkin pie spice
1	8 oz. package cream cheese, softened
1	14 oz. can Eagle Brand milk
1	16 oz. can pumpkin
½	t. salt
1	cup chopped nuts

Yield: 12-15 bars

Preheat oven to 350° In a large mixing bowl, on low speed, combine cake mix, 1 egg, butter and 2 teaspoons pumpkin pie spice until crumbly. Press into bottom of 13 x 9 pan. Set aside. In large mixing bowl, beat cheese until fluffy. Gradually beat in the remaining 2 teaspoons pumpkin pie spice, 2 eggs and salt; mix well. Mix in Eagle Brand milk, canned pumpkin, and pour over crust. Sprinkle nuts on top. Bake 30 to 40 minutes or longer until set. Cool, chill and cut into bars. Store in refrigerator.

Arnold Glasow observed,
"A loyal friend laughs at your jokes
when they're not so good
and sympathizes with your problems
when they're not so bad."' Herein, we consider the joys
of a good laugh and the blessings
of good friends to share it with.

Beef Stew
Cheesy Cornbread
Billie's Banana Pudding

Great menu for the first fall night

BEEF STEW

2	lbs. stew meat (cut into 1-inch cubes)
¼	cup peppered flour
2	T. oil
1	pkg. Schilling Beef Stew Seasoning mix
1½	t. salt
3	cups water
4	potatoes, quartered
4	carrots, cut into one-inch pieces
3	stalks celery, cut into one-inch pieces
1	onion, chopped
1	can stewed tomatoes

Yield: 6 1½-cup servings

Dredge stew meat with peppered flour. Brown on all sides in 2 T. oil in Dutch oven. Add seasoning mix, salt, and water. Cover and simmer 1½ hours or until meat is almost tender. Add vegetables. Cook 30 minutes longer. Thicken if desired.

Old Friends

It has been said that the best mirror is an old friend. But a lifelong pal is more than a mirror; he or she is also a priceless treasure. Thomas Edison said, "I have friends whose friendship I would not swap for the favor of all the kings of the world." We know how Edison felt.

CHEESY CORNBREAD

1½ cup chopped onion
¼ cup butter
1 cup sour cream
1 pkg sharp Cracker Barrel cheese, shredded
1 box Cinch Cornbread mix
1 egg
½ cup milk
1 medium can creamed corn
2 dashes Tabasco sauce

Yield: 12-15 servings

Simmer onion in butter. Mix this with sour cream and cheese. Combine cornbread mix, egg, milk, corn and Tabasco sauce. Put batter in 9½ x 13 inch baking dish. Pour onion mixture over batter. Follow cooking directions on Cinch box.

BILLIE'S BANANA PUDDING

Make sure you keep the kids out of the 'nilla wafers.

20-30 vanilla wafers
1 pkg. vanilla pudding and pie filling (4 serving size)
2 cups milk
1 T. butter or margarine
2 medium bananas, sliced

Yield: 8 servings

Line bottom and sides of 8-inch square or 1½ quart baking dish with wafers. Combine pudding mix, milk and butter in saucepan. Cook and stir over medium heat until mixture comes to a full boil. Remove from heat. Layer slices of banana over wafers, then add a layer of pudding. Repeat ending with pudding. Chill until firm, about three hours.

Hold a true friend with both hands.

African Proverb

FAB FIVE FOOTNOTES

Greasy soup: Drop in a lettuce leaf to absorb grease. Then remove leaf and discard.

Quick soup: Leftover roast and gravy is a great way to start soup. Just start adding vegetables, either leftover, frozen or fresh. Just let your imagination be your guide. Don't be afraid to try new seasonings.

Soup or stew too salty? Drop a peeled, quartered raw potato in and cook a few minutes. Remove potato, and taste the difference.

When cooking milk—to prevent sticking and boiling over, rinse the pot in cold water before starting.

To degrease meat soups and stews, put a sheet of waxed paper on top of the liquid before refrigerating. When ready to reheat, peel off the waxed paper and the fat will come off with it.

Chopped onions: Added to a casserole have best flavor if browned first.

No canned tomatoes? Try substituting 1 can tomato paste plus 1 cup water. Makes very little difference.

Remove the bitter taste from curry and chili powder by adding it to the recipe during the browning and not directly to the sauce.

NOTES

_____
_____
_____
_____
_____
_____
_____
_____
_____
_____
_____
_____
_____
_____
_____
_____
_____
_____
_____
_____
_____

COMPANY
COMIN'

*"To invite a person into your house
is to take charge of his happiness
for as long as he is under your roof."*

Brillat — Savarin

COMPANY COMIN'

These recipes are from our original monthly gatherings when we took turns entertaining each other in the grand style to celebrate our growing friendship. For us, delicious, beautifully displayed meals with specially chosen music has always created an atmosphere of sharing that nurtures openness and fond memories. We have made a commitment to lifelong friendship, and to keep that friendship a vital part of our separate worlds, we now get together four times a year for organized gatherings that include a celebration of fine food, themed events, and always music.

Whether its singing at the top of our lungs to Linda Ronstadt at Phyllis' fun dinners or listening to country music while Stephanie and Jan dance a seamless Texas two-step with no indication of who is leading. Our times together have always been shaped by music and have evolved into a bona fide music tradition we started on the trip to Carmel, California, when Debbie brought along Chris Isaack's CD *Baha Sessions*. As we were driving up the coast to Big Sur, we realized Isaack's music was perfect for our trip, and we played it over and over again. So it began: themed music for our outings with a final vote on the contenders for "most appropriate to the experience."

The Dixie Chicks' *Wide Open Spaces* fit the vastness of Buffalo Gap perfectly. Vonda Sheppard's songs were just right for deer patrol in Leakey, and Faith Hill's *Breathe* was the unanimous winner in the wonderful New Mexico air of Santa Fe.

Being women in our 40s, we appreciate music that is old or new, rock or country, and from many diverse artists. We listen to soft music while we drink our morning coffee, then crank up the rhythms as the day gets going. By evening we are rockin' out, dancing and singing in celebration of special times and special friendships.

We created these recipes for the best of company—for each other as honored guests in our respective homes; these events helped build deep bonds and seal our commitment to each other for a lifetime.

Hot Broccoli Dip
Jeff's Leg of Lamb
Stuffed Cabbage
Basic Creme Brulee

HOT BROCCOLI DIP

½   cup chopped onion
½   cup chopped celery
½   cup chopped mushrooms
3   T. butter
1   pkg. frozen broccoli,
     cooked & drained
1   can cream of mushroom
     soup
1   pkg. (16 oz.) garlic cheese,
     diced
Lemon juice
Garlic rounds

Yield: 6-8 servings

Sauté onion, celery and mushrooms in the butter in a double boiler. Then add the broccoli, mushroom soup and cheese. Melt to blend. Add a squeeze of lemon juice. Heat well before serving. May want to serve in a chafing dish. Best served with garlic rounds.

JEFF'S LEG OF LAMB

An excellent meat choice.

4-6   lbs. bone in leg of lamb
pepper (to taste)
garlic (to taste)
4   t. crushed rosemary

Season the lamb and place on a roasting rack in a pan. Cook at 325° for 30 to 35 minutes per pound.

STUFFED CABBAGE

Jeff's specialty—very good.

1   medium cabbage
½   lb. lettuce, steamed and finely chopped
½   lb. salt pork, rind removed, blanched five minutes, drained and finely chopped
¼   cup rice, cooked
¼   cup peas
3   T. olive oil
salt & pepper
1½-2 quarts beef or veal stock
1   garlic clove
1   bouquet garnish

Yield: 4 servings

Blanch the cabbage in salted water for 10 to 15 minutes until the outer leaves are just supple. Turn back the leaves of the cabbage and remove the heart. Finely chop the heart and squeeze out any excess water. Mix the chopped cabbage heart with the lettuce and the salt pork. Add the rice, peas, olive oil and seasoning. Put this mixture into the center of the cabbage and fold down the leaves to enclose it. Tie up the cabbage in a string net or cheesecloth and simmer in the stock for 2 to 3 hours. The garlic and bouquet garnish may be added to the cooking liquid according to taste. Remove the cabbage from the pan, untie the net or cheesecloth and serve the cabbage in a bowl.

BASIC CRÈME BRULEE

2 cups whipping cream
5 egg yolks
½ cup sugar
1 T. vanilla extract
½ cup firmly packed light
    brown sugar
garnishes: fresh raspberries,
    fresh mint sprigs

Yield: 5 servings

Combine first 4 ingredients, stirring with a wire whisk until sugar dissolves and mixture is smooth. Pour mixture evenly into 5 (5 x 1 inch) round individual baking dishes; place dishes in a large roasting pan or a 15 x 10 x 1 inch jelly roll pan. Prepare ½ inch water bath by pouring water into pan carefully not to water the creme brulee. (A water bath is simply a pan or jelly roll pan filled with water.

The water creates a cushion from the heat of the oven, allowing the custards to bake slowly without curdling.)

Bake at 275° for 45 to 50 minutes or until almost set. Cool custard in water in pan on a wire rack. Remove from pan, cover and refrigerate 8 hours or overnight.

Sprinkle about 1½ T. brown sugar evenly over each custard; place custards in jelly roll pan. Broil 5 inches from heat until brown sugar melts. Let stand 5 minutes to allow sugar to harden.

Note: a general rule if using 4, 6, or 8 oz. custard cups, bake the custards for 15 to 20 minutes longer. For 4 oz. cups you will get 10 servings. For 6 oz. you will get 7 servings and for 8 oz. you will get 4 servings.

"Crème Brulee can never be Jello!"
from My Best Friends Wedding

Garlic and Rosemary Beef Tenderloin
Seasoned Peppers and Onions
Potato-Onion Cakes
Raspberry Walnut Cake

Take the time to make this entire menu. The flavors blend beautifully. Just add your favorite green salad.

GARLIC AND ROSEMARY BEEF TENDERLOIN

The best marinade we have ever had!

½   cup olive oil
½   cup soy sauce
¼   cup balsamic vinegar or red wine vinegar
8   large garlic cloves, minced
4   t. dried rosemary, crumbled
1   4-6 lb. beef tenderloin, trimmed

Yield: 8 servings

Combine first 5 ingredients in glass baking dish. Add tenderloin and turn to coat. Season generously with pepper. Cover and refrigerate steak overnight, turning occasionally.

Bring steak to room temperature. Grill over hot coals or bake in the oven at 350° to an internal temperature of 125° (rare) to 150° (medium).

"Wrinkles only go where smiles have been."

Jimmy Buffet

SEASONED PEPPER AND ONIONS

⅓ cup olive oil
2 large onions, cut into
1-inch pieces
2 large red bell peppers,
cut into 1-inch pieces
1 green bell pepper,
cut into 1-inch pieces
¾ t. dried marjoram,
crumbled
⅛ t. dried crushed red
pepper

Yield: 8 servings

Heat oil in heavy large skillet over medium-high heat. Add onions and peppers, sauté until beginning to soften, about 8 minutes. Add marjoram and dried red pepper. Season to taste with salt and pepper and stir 2 minutes. Remove from heat.

POTATO-ONION CAKES

3 lbs. white potatoes
(about 6 large)
12 green onions (white and
green parts), chopped
salt and pepper
2 eggs
1 t. ground cumin
3 T. olive oil

Yield: 6 servings

Boil potatoes in large pot of water just until centers can be pierced with sharp knife, about 20 minutes. Drain. Cover and refrigerate until well chilled. (Can be prepared 1 day ahead.)

Peel potatoes. Using hand grater, coarsely grate potatoes into large bowl. Gently mix in green onions. Season to taste with salt and pepper. Beat eggs with cumin and gently mix into potato mixture. Form potatoes into 2½ inch-diameter cakes (about 1 inch thick). Cover and refrigerate until ready to cook. (Can be prepared 6 hours ahead.)

Heat 2 tablespoons oil in heavy large skillet over medium-high heat. Add potato cakes in batches and fry until golden brown, about 8 minutes per side, adding more oil as necessary.

RASPBERRY WALNUT CAKE

A favorite of the Fab Five.
Brings back memories of our Fredericksburg trip
and the Peach Tree Restaurant.

Cake:

5   extra large eggs, separated (use 6 eggs if necessary)
2   cups sugar, divided
1   cup butter
½   t. salt
1½   t. vanilla
1   t. baking soda
1   cup buttermilk
2   cups flour
1½   cups finely chopped, walnuts, divided
1   cup raspberry preserves, strained

For Frosting:

½   cup butter
12   oz. cream cheese
¼   cup raspberry preserves, strained
1½   t. vanilla
Approximately 1½ lbs powdered sugar

Yield: 10-12 servings

For Cake: Have all ingredients at room temperature. Using an electric mixer, beat egg whites until soft peaks form. Gradually add ½ cup sugar and beat until the consistency of meringue. Set aside.

Cream butter, the remaining sugar, salt and vanilla, adding egg yolks one at a time, until consistency of whipped cream. Stir baking soda into buttermilk.

Add this mixture alternately with flour to butter mixture, beginning and ending with flour.

Fold in egg white mixture and then add 1 cup walnuts. Pour batter into 3, 9 inch cake pans which have been greased and floured. Bake in preheated 325° oven for 40 minutes or until toothpick inserted in center comes out clean. Remove from oven and cool in pans for 5 to 10 minutes. Invert onto wire racks and cool completely.

On the first layer, spread ¼ cup preserves, then spread with a small amount of Raspberry Cream Cheese Frosting. Repeat with second layer.

Top with third layer. Frost top and sides with remaining cream cheese frosting. Carefully spread the remaining ½ cup preserves on the top of the cake. Sprinkle remaining ½ cup chopped walnuts on top of preserves.

Cake should be refrigerated if not eaten the day it is made.

For Raspberry Cream Cheese Frosting: Have all ingredients at room temperature. Using an electric mixer, cream together the butter, cream cheese, preserves and vanilla. Gradually add powdered sugar. Makes enough frosting for a 3 layer cake.

Mushroom Turnovers
Creamy Spinach Dip
Sweet and Sour Chicken and Shrimp
Tartly Frosted Lemon Squares

MUSHROOM TURNOVERS

2	packages refrigerated pie crust, thawed

Filling:
3	T. butter
1	large onion, finely chopped
¼	t. thyme
½	t. pepper
½	t. salt
2	T. flour
¼	cup sour cream
½	lb. fresh mushrooms, chopped
1	egg
1	t. milk

Yield: 15-20 servings

In a skillet heat butter. Add onion and brown. Add mushrooms; cook, stirring often, about 3 minutes. Add seasonings and sprinkle with flour. Stir in sour cream and cook gently until thickened.

COOL BEFORE NEXT STEP.

Roll out pie crust to press out creases. Cut 3 inches rounds (as many as possible) with a biscuit cutter.

Place ½ to ¾ teaspoon of mixture on each round, fold dough in half. Press edges with fork. Place on greased cookie sheet. Brush top with 1 egg slightly beaten with 1 t. milk. Bake at 450° 10-15 minutes or until lightly browned.

May be frozen before baking.

CREAMY SPINACH DIP

8 oz. sour cream
1 cup mayonnaise
½ t. celery salt
½ t. dill weed
¼ t. onion salt
¼ cup chopped green onions
3 cups frozen cut leaf spinach, thawed, well-drained
8 oz. can water chestnuts drained, finely chopped
3 T. chopped red bell pepper, if desired

Yield: 3½ cups

In medium bowl, combine sour cream, mayonnaise and seasonings. Stir in onions, spinach, water chestnuts and red pepper. Cover; refrigerate to blend flavors.

Serve with crisp vegetable dippers, assorted crackers or bread.

SWEET AND SOUR SHRIMP AND CHICKEN

¼ cup firmly packed brown sugar
2 T. cornstarch
¾ t. ground ginger
¼ t. garlic powder
¼ t. curry powder
1 T. Worcestershire sauce
1½ cups pineapple juice
⅓ cup wine vinegar
¼ cup catsup
1½ lbs. medium-size fresh shrimp, unpeeled
1 T. butter or margarine, melted
1 T. olive oil
2 cups cubed cooked chicken (about 3 breast halves)

1 cup unsalted cashew nuts
Hot cooked rice

Yield: 6 servings

Combine first 9 ingredients in a medium saucepan. Cook over medium heat 5 minutes or until thickened and clear, stirring frequently. Set aside.

Peel and devein shrimp. Sauté shrimp in butter and olive oil in a large skillet 3 minutes. Add chicken and cashew nuts; sauté an additional 2 minutes. Add sauce to shrimp mixture and cook until thoroughly heated, stirring occasionally. Serve over rice.

TARTLY FROSTED LEMON SQUARES

3 ½ oz. can flake coconut
2 eggs, separated
1 can eagle brand milk
⅓ cup fresh lemon juice
¼ cup butter, melted
¼ cup flour
½ t. salt

Frosting:
1 cup confectioners' sugar
2 T. butter, melted
1 T. fresh lemon juice

Yield: 8 servings

Preheat oven to 350°. Pat coconut on bottom of 9 x 9 baking dish and set aside. In a large mixing bowl beat egg yolks, stir in milk, lemon juice and butter. Beat until smooth. Stir in flour and salt. In a small bowl beat egg whites to peak. Fold into egg yolk mixture. Pour into pan. Bake 25-30 minutes.

Once cooled, cut into squares. Mix confectioner sugar, melted butter and lemon juice until smooth. Spread on top of each square.

"There is no sight on earth more appealing than the sight of a woman making dinner for someone she loves."

Beef Marengo with Buttered Noodles
Zesty Tuna Dip
Spinach-Stuffed Squash
Strawberry Puff

BEEF MARENGO WITH BUTTERED NOODLES

1	4 lb. boneless chuck roast
½	cup vegetable oil
1	cup onion, chopped
1	cup celery, chopped
1	clove garlic, crushed
1	cup dry white wine
2	8 oz. cans tomato sauce
2	bay leaves
1	t. dried whole oregano
½	t. dried whole rosemary
½	t. salt
½	t. pepper
1	T. fresh parsley, chopped
1	lb. fresh mushrooms, sliced
2	T. lemon juice
¼	cup butter
1	T. flour
2	T. water
1	8 oz. package egg noodles
¼	cup melted butter

Yield: 8-10 servings

Trim excess fat from roast; cut into 1 inch cubes. Brown meat in hot oil in a large Dutch oven; remove meat. Add onion, celery and garlic to pan drippings; sauté until tender. Add meat, ½ cup wine and the next 7 ingredients to vegetable mixture; bring to a boil. Cover, reduce heat and simmer one hour or until meat is tender, stirring occasionally. Discard bay leaves.

Combine mushrooms and lemon juice, tossing gently. Melt butter in a large skillet; add mushrooms and sauté until tender.

Combine flour and 2 tablespoons water, stir until smooth. Stir flour mixture and sautéed mushrooms and remaining ½ cup wine into meat mixture.

Cover and cook over medium heat 15 minutes. Transfer mixture to chafing dish; sprinkle with chopped parsley, if desire.

Serve over buttered egg noodles.

ZESTY TUNA DIP

1	can tuna
1½	cups sour cream
2	t. lemon juice
3	T. picante sauce
1	package Good Seasons Italian dressing mix
1	hard boiled egg, mashed

Yield: 6 appetizer servings

Mix all ingredients together. Serve with giant Fritos.

SPINACH-STUFFED SQUASH

8	medium-size yellow squash
1	chicken-flavored bouillon cube
1	10 oz. package frozen chopped spinach
¼	cup cottage cheese
1	T. Parmesan cheese
1	large egg, beaten
¼	t. seasoned salt
¼	t. coarsely ground black pepper
3	T. dry breadcrumbs
Paprika	
Vegetable cooking spray	

Yield: 8 servings

Wash squash thoroughly. Drop in boiling water with bouillon cube; cover and simmer 8-10 minutes or until tender but still firm. Drain and cool slightly; cut squash in half lengthwise. Scoop out pulp, leaving firm shells; mash pulp. Cook spinach according to package; drain well and add to squash pulp. Add cottage cheese and mix well. Stir in next 5 ingredients; spoon into squash shells. Sprinkle squash with breadcrumbs and paprika. Place on baking sheet sprayed with cooking spray; cover with foil and bake at 325° for 30 minutes.

STRAWBERRY PUFF

1   16 oz. package frozen
    whole strawberries,
    partially thawed
2   egg whites
¼   cup sugar
1   T. lemon juice
1   cup frozen whipped
    topping, thawed
1   cup frozen whole
    strawberries, partially
    thawed

Yield: 8 servings

Combine first 4 ingredients in a large mixing bowl. Beat at high speed 10-12 minutes or until stiff peaks form. Add whipped topping; beat until smooth. Spoon into individual serving dishes and freeze until firm.

Crush remaining strawberries with a fork.

Spoon over dessert.

"One cannot think well, love well, sleep well, if one has not dined well."

Virginia Wolf

Easy Caesar Salad

Beef Tenderloin with Mushrooms

Chive Potato Pancakes

Toffee Meringue Torte

EASY CAESAR SALAD

2	heads romaine lettuce
¾	cup olive oil
¼	cup vegetable oil
4	cloves garlic, halved
1	cup white bread cubes (about ¼ inch squares)
2	eggs
Juice of 1 large lemon	
¼	t. Worcestershire sauce
½	t. salt
½	t. freshly ground pepper
¼	cup freshly grated Parmesan cheese

Yield: 8 servings

Wash romaine; trim core and separate stalk into individual leaves. Discard wilted or discolored portion. Drain, then place romaine on a dry towel, roll gently to dry thoroughly. Place in a plastic bag. Chill lettuce 8 hours or overnight.

Combine olive oil, vegetable oil, and garlic in a jar with a tight-fitting lid. Let stand several hours.

Place bread cubes in a 15 × 10 × 1 inch jellyroll pan. Sprinkle about 3 tablespoons of oil mixture over cubes; toss gently to coat. Bake at 250° for 15 minutes or until dry and crisp; cool. Store in an airtight container.

Before combining salad, coddle eggs by bringing water to a boil in a small saucepan; turn heat off. Carefully lower eggs (in the shell) into water, using a slotted spoon; let stand 1 minute. Remove eggs from water; set aside to cool.

Cut coarse ribs from large leaves of romaine; tear leaves into bite-size pieces, and place in a large salad bowl. Discard garlic slices from olive oil mixture. Add the coddled eggs, lemon juice, Worcestershire sauce, salt, and pepper to oil. Cover and shake vigorously. Pour over romaine lettuce, and toss to coat. Sprinkle with grated Parmesan cheese and top with croutons. Serve immediately.

BEEF TENDERLOIN WITH MUSHROOMS

1   lb. fresh mushrooms, sliced
1   cup green onion, chopped
¼   cup butter or margarine, melted
¼   cup fresh parsley, chopped
1   6-7 lb. beef tenderloin
½   t. seasoned salt
¼   t. lemon pepper seasoning
1   4 oz. package crumbled blue cheese
1   8 oz. bottle red wine vinegar and oil dressing
Crushed peppercorns

Yield: 8-10 servings

Sauté sliced mushrooms and green onions in butter in a large skillet until tender; drain. Stir in parsley and set mixture aside.

Trim excess fat from beef tenderloin. Cut tenderloin lengthwise to within ¼ inch of the tenderloin edge, leaving one long side connected. Sprinkle with seasoned salt and lemon pepper seasoning. Spoon mushroom mixture into opening of tenderloin; sprinkle with blue cheese. Fold top side over stuffing. Tie tenderloin securely with heavy string at 2-inch intervals. Place tenderloin in a large, shallow dish. Pour dressing over tenderloin; cover and refrigerate 8 hours, basting with marinade occasionally.

Remove tenderloin from marinade. Press crushed peppercorns onto each side of the tenderloin. Grill over medium-hot coals, covered or tented, 35 minutes or until meat thermometer registers 140° (rare) to 160° (medium). Transfer to platter, remove string and slice to serve.

Tenderloin may be baked at 350° for 40 minutes or until meat thermometer registers 140°-160°.

Chive Potato Pancakes

4	cups cooked mashed potatoes
2	eggs, beaten
4	T. buttermilk
3	T. chopped fresh chives
1	t. salt
¼	t. white pepper
1½	cups crushed round buttery cracker crumbs (about 40 crackers)
¼	cup butter or margarine, melted
½	t. paprika
Chives (optional)	

Yield: 8 servings

Combine first 6 ingredients; mix well. Divide mixture into 8 portions, and shape into pancakes; roll in cracker crumbs. Place flat on a lightly greased pan; cover and refrigerate up to 24 hours.

Combine butter and paprika; drizzle over pancakes. Bake at 375° for 20 to 25 minutes or until golden. Garnish pancakes with chives, if desired.

Potato Pancakes may be frozen. To bake from a frozen state, place pancakes on a greased baking sheet. Combine butter and paprika; drizzle over pancakes. Bake at 375° for 35 minutes or until golden.

*"Live Life to the Fullest. You have to color outside the lines
if you want to make your life a masterpiece.
Laugh some everyday. Keep growing, keep dreaming,
follow your heart. The important thing is
not to stop questioning."*

Albert Einstein

TOFFEE MERINGUE TORTE

4   egg whites, room
     temperature
1   t. vinegar
1   cup sugar
1   t. vanilla extract
6   1.1 oz. English toffee-
     flavored candy bars,
     frozen then crushed
2   cups whipping cream,
     whipped
Chocolate curls (optional)

Yield: 8-10 servings

Grease bottom of two 8 inch round cakepans, line with brown paper and grease paper. Beat egg whites at high speed with electric mixer until foamy. Add vinegar and sugar; continue beating until soft peaks form. Stir in vanilla. Spoon meringue into prepared pans. Bake at 275° for 2 hours. Remove layers from pans and paper from layers. Cool on wire racks.

Gently fold crushed candy into whipped cream. Spread whipped cream frosting between layers and on top and side of meringue layers. Cover loosely and chill 8 hours or overnight. Garnish with chocolate curls, if desired.

"All's well that ends with a good meal."

Arnold Lobel

The Jones' Family Salad
Chicken Breasts and Linguine with Creamy Green Onion Sauce
Fresh Strawberry Tart

THE JONES' FAMILY SALAD

3   firm heads Bibb lettuce
3   slices crisp bacon, crumbled
1   hard-boiled egg, chopped

Dressing
¼   cup cider vinegar
½   t. salt
6   drops Tabasco sauce
1   t. Dijon-style mustard
Juice of 1 lemon
6   twists freshly ground black pepper
1   t. finely diced red bell pepper
¾   cup sunflower oil
½   t. chopped fresh chives

Yield: 10 servings

Separate leaves from lettuce heads carefully and soak in very cold water until crisp; drain. Wash lettuce thoroughly and dry on paper towel or in a salad spinner.

In a metal mixing bowl, stir together vinegar, salt, Tabasco sauce, mustard, lemon juice, ground pepper and diced pepper, using a wire whisk.

Gradually add oil, beating constantly, until dressing is thickened. Add chives and stir.

Transfer dry lettuce leaves to a large mixing bowl. Add ¼ cup of the dressing and toss lightly using salad forks. (Extra salad dressing may be kept for several days in the refrigerator, but it should be served at room temperature.)

Divide salad among 10 individual salad plates. Sprinkle with crumbled bacon and chopped egg, and serve at once.

Chicken Breasts and Linguine with Creamy Green Onion Sauce

2   T. butter
5 to 6 boneless chicken breast
    halves, skinned
Salt and freshly ground pepper
2   large shallots or green
    onions, minced
½   cup chicken broth
2   cups whipping cream
1¼   cups freshly grated
    Romano cheese
1   bunch green onions,
    chopped
¾   lb. green linguine or
    fettuccine
2   T. butter, room temperature
Freshly grated Romano cheese

Yield: 4-6 servings

Melt 2 tablespoons butter in heavy large skillet over medium-low heat. Season chicken with salt and pepper. Add to skillet and sauté until cooked through, turning occasionally, about 12 minutes. Transfer to heated plate and tent with foil to keep warm.

Add shallots to same skillet and stir 1 minute. Add broth, increase heat and boil until reduced to glaze, about 5 minutes. Add cream and boil until slightly thickened, stirring occasionally, about 5 minutes. Add 1¼ cups Romano and green onions and stir until cheese melts and sauce thickens, adding juices accumulated on chicken plate. Season generously with pepper.

Meanwhile, cook linguine in large pot of rapidly boiling salted water, stirring occasionally to prevent sticking. Drain well. Transfer to large heated bowl. Add 2 tablespoons butter and mix until butter melts.

Thinly slice chicken on diagonal and arrange atop pasta. Pour sauce over chicken and pasta. Serve immediately, passing cheese separately.

FRESH STRAWBERRY TART

½ cup cold butter
1½ cups flour
¼ t. salt
2 T. sugar
1 egg
⅔ cup semisweet chocolate chips
2 quarts fresh strawberries
½ cup strawberry jam

Yield: 8 servings

Cut the butter into pieces. In a food processor, combine the flour, salt, sugar and butter and pulse until the mixture resembles coarse meal. Beat the egg into mixture, add it to the flour mixture and process until the dough forms a ball. With your fingers, press the dough into an 11 inch tart or pie pan. Chill the shell in the refrigerator for at least 20 minutes. Heat the oven to 375°. Prick the bottom and sides of the shell thoroughly with a fork. Press a double thickness of aluminum foil against the shell and bake for 15 minutes. Remove the foil and continue baking until golden, 10 to 15 minutes. Let the pastry cool. Melt the chocolate chips over simmering water or in a microwave oven at medium for 2 minutes. Spread the chocolate over the bottom of the cooked shell. Cut a thin slice off the stem end of each strawberry and arrange the berries, points up, on the warm chocolate. Melt the strawberry jam over low heat and strain it. Thin the jam with 1 to 2 teaspoons of water if it is too thick for glazing. Brush the strawberries with the warm jam. Serve the tart with whipped cream if desired. (Tart should be assembled the day it's served, but the crust can be made ahead.)

Spring Salad
Beef Wellington with Mushroom Sauce
Zucchini-Pepper Skillet
Salted Peanut Cake with Milk Chocolate Frosting

SPRING SALAD

4	hard-boiled eggs
3	T. vegetable oil
1½	t. sugar
¾	t. salt
¼	t. dry mustard
⅛	t. pepper
3	T. cider vinegar
⅓	cup milk
2½	cups torn iceberg lettuce (1 small head)
2½	cups torn escarole (1 small head)
1	cup shredded carrots
2	T. finely chopped onion

Yield: 6 servings

Separate egg whites and yolks. Slice egg whites; set aside. Mash egg yolks; add vegetable oil, sugar, salt, mustard, and pepper. Slowly stir in cider vinegar; mix well. Gradually add milk, and mix well. Refrigerate. Combine remaining ingredients and sliced egg whites; refrigerate.

Just before serving, pour dressing mixture over salad; toss gently.

"What I am most attracted to in my friends are their spirits: they are people who love life, who are passionate, who take risks to live fully, who are sensitive to feelings and idiosyncrasies, who share this goodness with me."

Alexandra Stoddard

BEEF WELLINGTON
Individual servings

1   box Pepperidge Farm
    pastry sheets,
    room temperature
4   4 oz. beef filets
1   garlic clove, halved
salt and pepper to taste
½   stick butter
4   T. Brandy (optional)
½-¾ cup fresh mushrooms,
    chopped finely in
    processor
1   4 oz. tin of liver pate
    (maybe less)

Yield: 4 servings

Rub filets with garlic; salt and pepper then sauté in butter 3 to 4 minutes each side. Flame Brandy and pour over filets. Remove filets and chill.

Sauté mushrooms (use same pan) and chill. Mix liver pate with mushrooms. Spread mixture over top of filets and refrigerate.

Cut pastry into appropriate square size. Place filet, pate side down, fold dough up and seal with butter. Place seam down on greased cookie sheet. Brush with lightly beaten egg.

Can be made days before and frozen. Allow to thaw completely before baking. Or preassemble and chill the night before. Bring to room temperature and bake.

Bake at 425° for 20 to 25 minutes.

MUSHROOM SAUCE

¼   cup minced onion
3   T. flour
1   10 oz. can beef broth
salt and pepper to taste
6   large mushrooms, sliced
½   cup red wine
1   bay leaf
1   t. Worcestershire sauce
2   T. butter
dash of red wine (used for
    sautéing)

Yield: 4 servings

Sauté onions and mushrooms in butter and dash of red wine. Stir in flour; add ½ cup red wine, broth and bay leaf. Stir until sauce bubbles and thickens— about 20 minutes.

Season with salt, pepper and Worcestershire sauce. Serve filets with sauce on top.

77

ZUCCHINI-PEPPER SKILLET

1	pound zucchini (about 4 small)
1	onion, thinly sliced
1	small green pepper, chopped
2	T. vegetable oil
1	clove garlic, crushed
1	t. salt
⅛	t. pepper
2	tomatoes, cut into wedges
parsley (for garnish)	
½	cup shredded Parmesan cheese (optional)

Yield: 4 servings

Wash squash; remove stem and blossom ends. Cut into ¼ inch slices or cubes. Cook and stir zucchini, onion, green pepper, oil, garlic, salt and pepper in 10 inch skillet until heated through. Cover and cook over medium heat, stirring occasionally, until vegetables are crisp-tender, about 5 minutes.

Add tomatoes. Cover and cook over low heat just until tomatoes are heated through, about 3 minutes. Sprinkle with snipped parsley and grated Parmesan cheese if desired.

(For Yellow Squash Skillet: Substitute 1 pound yellow summer squash, about 2 medium for the zucchini and 1 t. ground ginger for the garlic. Omit the pepper.)

"Don't undermine your worth by comparing yourself with others. It is because we are different that each of us is special."

Nancye Sims

SALTED PEANUT CAKE WITH MILK CHOCOLATE FROSTING

Peanuts and milk chocolate are a perfect match in this old-fashioned cake.

Cake:

1⅔ cups salted red-skinned Spanish peanuts
2⅓ cups cake flour
1 T. baking powder
¾ cup (1½ sticks) unsalted butter (room temperature)
1½ cups sugar
2 t. vanilla extract
4 large eggs, room temperature
1½ cups milk, room temperature

Frosting:

1 lb. milk chocolate, chopped
1½ sticks unsalted butter, room temperature
3 large eggs, room temperature

Yield: 12 servings

For cake: Preheat oven to 350°. Grease and flour two 9 x 2 inch cake pans. Place peanuts in a plastic bag and crush into ⅛ to ¼ inch pieces using a rolling pin. Sift flour and baking powder into a small bowl. Using an electric mixer, cream butter with sugar and vanilla in a large bowl. Add eggs one at a time, beating well after each addition. Beat mixture until light and fluffy. Beat in flour mixture and milk alternately, beginning and ending with flour. Add peanuts and beat just until batter is combined.

Divide batter between prepared pans. Bake until cakes pull away from sides of the pans and tops are deep golden brown, about 40 minutes. Cool cakes in pans on rack 10 minutes. Invert cakes onto racks. Turn right side up and cool completely. (Can be prepared one day ahead. Wrap cake layers in plastic and store at room temperature.)

For frosting: Melt chocolate in top of double boiler over barely simmering water, stirring until smooth. Cool slightly. Using an electric mixer, beat butter and eggs in a large bowl until well blended. Gradually add chocolate and beat until frosting forms soft peaks, stopping occasionally to scrape down bowl. If frosting is too soft to spread, beat briefly over a bowl of ice water.

Place one cake layer flat side up on a serving platter. Spread with 1¼ cups frosting. Cover with second cake layer, flat side down. Spread 1¼ cups frosting on sides of cake. Spread remaining frosting over top of cake in swirl pattern. (Can be prepared 4 hours ahead.)

Leslie's Beef Bonaparte
Not the Same Seven Layered Salad
Corn Casserole
Kahlua Smoothies

LESLIE'S BEEF BONAPARTE

1	pound ground beef, browned
1	16 oz. can tomatoes, drained but reserve juices
2	t. garlic juice
2	t. sugar
2	t. salt or 1 t. if using garlic salt
1	package Mozarella cheese
1	5 oz. package thin egg noodles
6	green onions, chopped
8	oz. sour cream
1	cup grated Cheddar cheese
1	bay leaf

cracked pepper to taste
Tabasco to taste

Yield: 6 servings

Brown beef, drain well and add the tomatoes but not the juices. Brown tomatoes lightly and add juice. Season with garlic juice, sugar, salt and Tabasco. Stir and lower heat to simmer. Sprinkle with cracked pepper and add the bay leaf snipped in two. Let this simmer for 30 minutes. Cook the noodles, drain and combine with chopped green onions and sour cream. Grease a 9 x 13 glass dish. Layer the noodles, then meat mixture, then top with the Cheddar cheese. Cook covered for 40 minutes at 350°. The last five minutes remove foil and add a layer of Mozarella cheese. Cook until cheese is melted.

This freezes great.

NOT THE SAME SEVEN LAYERED SALAD

*Our sweet friend Eddie always serves this
in a big glass bowl.*

2   cups fresh spinach,
     torn into pieces
6 to 8 slices of bacon, fried,
     drained and chopped
4   hard-boiled eggs, sliced
salt and pepper to taste
½   head of lettuce, sliced thin
1   package frozen peas,
     uncooked but thawed
1½   bunches of green onions,
     including tops and
     bottoms, sliced
1   small can roasted red
     peppers, chopped
6 to 8 ounces Feta cheese,
     crumbled

Dressing:
1   cup real mayonnaise
1   cup salad dressing
Mix two ingredients together.

Yield: 8-12 servings

Layer ingredients as given
above. Add dressing and top
with Feta cheese. Refrigerate for
at least 24 hours. Keeps for days.

CORN CASSEROLE

8   ounce cream cheese
3   T. butter
¼   cup milk
2   small cans white corn
1   small can chopped green
     chilies
3 big shakes of Tabasco
salt and pepper to taste

Yield: 4-6 servings

Melt cream cheese, butter and
milk. Add the corn, chopped
green chilies, Tabasco, salt and
pepper. Bake in small casserole
dish at 350° for 30 minutes.

KAHLUA SMOOTHIES

1   pint vanilla ice cream
⅓   cup cream de Cacao
⅓   cup Kahlua

Yield: 2½ cups

Mix in blender

Salad with Creamy Mustard Dressing
Chicken and Crab Supreme
Squash Soufflé
Easy Dinner Rolls
Napoleons

SALAD WITH CREAMY MUSTARD DRESSING

2	hard boiled eggs, mashed
1½	t. salt
1½	t. sugar
1	t. coarse black pepper
1	T. chopped parsley
1	T. Dijon mustard
1	large clove garlic, crushed
½	cup olive oil
5	T. heavy cream
¼	cup wine vinegar

Yield: approximately 1 cup of dressing

Blend ingredients, one by one in the order given. Toss with your favorite greens. (We recommend a combination of fresh spinach and butter lettuce.)

"Know Your Passion, Show Your Passion"

"Your interests, wishes, and happiness determine what you actually do well, more then intelligence, aptitudes or skills do."

Richard Bolles

CHICKEN AND CRAB SUPREME

6   whole chicken breast
salt and pepper
3   T. butter
1/3   cup minced onion
3/4   cup chopped mushrooms
5   T. dry vermouth or sherry
     or white wine
6 to 8 oz. crab meat
1/2   cup herb seasoned stuffing
     mix
1   egg, slightly beaten
5   T. flour
1   T. paprika
2   T. butter, melted
4   oz. grated Swiss cheese
paprika (for garnish)
parsley (for garnish)

Sauce Supreme:

4   T. butter
4   T. flour
1 1/2   cups chicken broth
1   cup heavy cream
1/2   cup dry vermouth, sherry
     or white wine
salt and pepper
pinch of nutmeg
2   egg yolks

Yield: 6 servings

Skin and bone breasts. Pound thin; salt and pepper. Sauté onion in 3 tablespoons butter until soft. Add mushrooms and sauté for another 2 minutes. Add wine, crabmeat, stuffing and egg. Mix well. If too moist, add a bit more stuffing mix. Divide into 6 portions and sandwich between breast.

Mix flour and paprika. Roll breast in the flour-paprika mixture and place in greased baking dish. Drizzle with 2 tablespoons melted butter. Cover and bake at 375° for 45 minutes. Remove any excess juices. (The chicken breast may be cooled at this point and refrigerated.)

Sauce Supreme: Melt butter and stir in flour for 2 minutes. Add 1 cup broth and wine; cook until thickened. Add cream and cook for 1 minute. Add additional broth, if necessary, to make a medium thick sauce. Add salt, pepper and nutmeg. Taste for seasoning. Beat yolks in small bowl and add some of the hot sauce to them, to slowly warm the yolks, then add the rest of the sauce. Do not boil or the sauce will curdle. Press plastic wrap over the top of the sauce to keep skin from forming. Refrigerate.

To assemble: Heat sauce in the top of a double boiler. Cover chicken breast with sauce, a sprinkle of cheese and last 2 tablespoons of melted butter. Return to 375° oven for about 15 minutes to heat through. Place under hot broiler to glaze top (only until cheese melts) just before serving. Garnish with chopped parsley and paprika.

SQUASH SOUFFLÉ

¼	cup finely chopped onions
4	T. butter
4	pounds yellow squash
1½	cups fine bread crumbs
4	T. chopped pimentos (optional)
1	T. salt
¼	t. pepper
2	eggs, beaten

Yield: 8 servings

Cook squash in boiling salted water until mushy (about 20 minutes). Drain and mash. Sauté the onion in butter until tender. Add sautéed onion and the rest of the ingredients to the mashed squash, add the eggs last. Beat thoroughly. Pour into a well buttered casserole dish. Bake for 30 minutes at 350°.

EASY DINNER ROLLS

1	package dry yeast
¼	cup warm water
1	cup milk
½	cup butter
1	t. salt
4	cups flour
2	eggs, room temperature

Yield: 2 dozen

Dissolve yeast in water. Scald milk, add butter and salt. Cool. Add flour, a little at a time. Add yeast. Beat in eggs. Cover. Let rise until double in bulk. Punch down and shape into rolls. Bake at 350° for 25 to 30 minutes. Dough will keep in refrigerator.

"Friendship is the only cement that will ever hold the world together."

Woodrow Wilson

NAPOLEONS

PUFF PASTRY

Puff Pastry—You can make your own puff pastry following the recipe, but it is very time consuming. We recommend Pepperidge Farm puff pastry, as an alternative.

Homemade Puff Pastry:

1	cup butter
1¾	cups flour, sifted
½	cup very cold water

Chill 1 cup butter. Reserve 2 tablespoons, chill. Work remaining chilled butter with back of wooden spoon just until pliable. Pat or roll between sheets of waxed paper to 8 × 6 inch rectangle. Chill at least 1 hour in refrigerator or 20 minutes in the freezer. (good to chill utensils before each use.)

Cut reserved 2 T. butter into the sifted flour until mixture resembles coarse meal. Gradually add cold water, tossing with fork to make stiff dough. Shape into ball. Knead on lightly floured surface until smooth and elastic, about 5 minutes. Cover dough and let rest 10 minutes.

On lightly floured surface, roll dough in 15 × 9 inch rectangle. (Roll from center just to edges.) Brush off excess flour; fold in thirds, then turn dough and fold in thirds again. Press edges to seal. Wrap and chill at least 1 hour. Repeat rolling, folding and chilling 2 or 3 times more. Shape Napoleons in 16, 3½ × 2 inch rectangles.

Store bought Puff Pastry:

Roll Puff Pastry into 14 × 8 inch rectangle, ⅜ inch thick. Cut off all edges. Prick dough well with fork. Cut in 16, 3½ × 2 inch rectangles. Place on baking sheets covered with 3 or 4 thicknesses of paper towels. Chill well. Brush with mixture of 1 slightly beaten egg white and 1 tablespoon ice water.

Bake at 450° for 6 minutes, then at 300° for 25 to 30 minutes, until lightly browned and crisp. Remove from pan, cool on rack. (If baked ahead, place on baking sheet covered with 4 thicknesses of paper towels, heat at 300° for about 10 minutes.)

(Continued on Next Page)

FRENCH CUSTARD FILLING:

⅓ cup sugar	In saucepan, combine sugar,
1 T. all-purpose flour	flour, cornstarch and salt.
1 T. cornstarch	Gradually stir in milk. Cook and
¼ t. salt	stir 2 to 3 minutes longer. Stir a
1½ cup milk	little hot mixture into egg yolk;
1 egg yolk, slightly beaten	return to hot mixture. Cook and
1 t. vanilla	stir until mixture just boils. Add
½ cup whipping cream, whipped	vanilla, cool. Beat smooth, fold in whipped cream.

CHOCOLATE GLAZE:

½ cup milk chocolate or ¼ cup semisweet chocolate, melted
¼ t. vanilla
boiling water (to make drizzle)

Yield: 16

Combine all ingredients.

ASSEMBLING THE NAPOLEONS:

Separate each pastry into 3 layers. Top each layer with French Custard Filling. Each Napoleon has 3 layers of pastry and 2 layers of custard. Glaze the top layer with chocolate glaze.

Spicy Shrimp Dip
Veal Paprika
Salad with Sesame Seed Dressing
Chocolate Kahlua Cake

SPICY SHRIMP DIP

8   oz. cream cheese, room
    temperature
1   cup sour cream
1   envelope dry Italian
    dressing (we recommend
    Good Seasons)
1   lb. shrimp; boiled, peeled
    and deveined
1   T. mayonnaise
3   t. Tabasco
1   t. horseradish
1   t. lemon juice

Yield: 6 appetizer servings

Put shrimp in food processor to chop finely. Mix all ingredients together and refrigerate. Allow flavors to blend several hours before serving. Serve with assorted crackers.

VEAL PAPRIKA

¼   cup tissue-thin sliced
     onions
3   T. butter
1   lb. Veal cutlets, sliced
     ¼ inch thick and cut in
     ¼ lb. portions
¼   cup flour
1   t. salt
⅛   t. pepper
1½   cups chicken broth
¾   cup sour cream
1   t. paprika

Yield: 4 servings

Sauté onion in butter until soft. Remove onion and then brown cutlets that have been rolled in seasoned flour (flour, salt and pepper). Add broth and onions and simmer, covered for 1 hour. Add sour cream and paprika and cook slowly until well blended. Serve with buttered noodles or rice.

SESAME SEED DRESSING

1	cup sugar
1	t. paprika
½	t. dry mustard
1	t. salt
1	t. Worcestershire sauce
1	T. onion juice
2	cups vegetable oil
1	cup cider vinegar
½	cup toasted sesame seeds

Red and green salad greens
Red onion, thinly sliced

Put sugar, seasonings and onion juice in a bowl and beat until thoroughly combined. Add the oil very gradually, then the vinegar, a little at a time. Keep in a covered jar in the refrigerator. To toast sesame seeds, place on a shallow pan or baking sheet in 300° oven; watch closely and stir frequently. They should be just golden brown to bring out the flavor, but will become bitter if toasted until they are dark. Add toasted seeds last.

This dressing is great served on a mixed red and green leaf salad and then topped with thinly sliced red onions.

CHOCOLATE KAHLUA CAKE

Easy and delicious!

1	package chocolate cake mix
4	eggs
¾	cup Kahlua
1	package (6 oz.) instant chocolate pudding mix
½	cup vegetable oil
½	cup water
6	T. Kahlua
1	cup confectioners sugar, sifted

Yield: 10 servings

Preheat oven to 350°. Combine first 6 ingredients in mixing bowl and blend well. Pour into greased and lightly floured 10 inch fluted tube pan. Bake 45 to 50 minutes or until cake springs back when lightly touched. Combine Kahlua and confectioners sugar. While cake is still warm in pan, poke holes in cake: pour liqueur mixture over. Allow cake to cool in pan at least 2 hours before removing.

*Chicken Breast Parmesan
with Italian Sauce*

Italian Vegetables

Pull Away Bread

Killer Strawberry Cheesecake

CHICKEN BREAST PARMESAN

Recommend serving over your favorite pasta.

4	chicken breast, pounded
1	clove garlic, pressed
¼	cup olive oil
1	cup Italian breadcrumbs
¼	cup Parmesan cheese
4	slices mozzarella cheese
1	package angel hair pasta

Italian Sauce (see recipe below)

Yield: 4 servings

Brown chicken breast in olive oil and garlic. Mix together breadcrumbs and Parmesan; add chicken breast to coat. Lay in a glass dish and cover with the Italian sauce. Cover with foil. Bake one hour at 350°. Take the foil off and add mozzarella cheese. Bake 10 more minutes. Serve over pasta.

ITALIAN SAUCE

2	8 oz. cans tomato sauce
1	T. Italian seasoning
¼	t. sugar
¼	t. garlic powder

salt and pepper to taste

Heat to warm the tomato sauce and add the seasonings.

89

ITALIAN VEGETABLES

2   yellow squash,
    sliced thin
2   zucchini, sliced thin
1   can stewed Italian
    tomatoes
1   clove garlic, pressed
1   T. Italian Seasoning

Yield: 4 servings

Steam vegetables until al dente. In a saucepan, add stewed tomatoes to the vegetables. Season with garlic and Italian seasoning. Simmer.

PULL AWAY BREAD

¼   cup grated Parmesan
    cheese
3   T. sesame seeds
1   t. dried basil
1   25 oz. package frozen roll
    dough, unthawed
3   T. butter, melted

Yield: 8 servings

Stir together first 3 ingredients; sprinkle ⅓ of mixture into a buttered 12 cup Bundt pan.

Place half of frozen rolls in pan; drizzle with half of butter and sprinkle with half of remaining cheese mixture. Repeat procedure with remaining frozen rolls, butter and cheese mixture.

Let rise in a warm place free from drafts, 3 to 4 hours or until doubled in bulk.

Bake at 350° for 30 minutes shielding with aluminum foil after 20 minutes to prevent excessive browning. Loosen bread from sides of pan with a knife; immediately invert onto a serving plate.

KILLER STRAWBERRY CHEESECAKE

A favorite dessert of Diane and Debbie's since our college days at Texas Tech University. One of the best cheesecakes around!

Crust:
2½ cups vanilla wafer crumbs
½ cup chopped pecans
1 stick butter, melted

Mix together vanilla wafer crumbs, pecans and butter. Press into springform pan.

Filling:
4 eggs
1½ cup sugar
2 t. vanilla
3 8 oz. packages cream cheese, softened

Yield: 10-12 servings

Mix filling ingredients together and beat until smooth. Spoon over crust. Bake at 325° for 45-60 minutes. (When shaken it should be firm.)

Topping:
1 pint sour cream
1 cup sugar
3 oz. package strawberry jello
1 16 oz. package frozen strawberries

Mix together sour cream and sugar. Pour over baked mixture (while still hot) and bake 15 minutes longer. Let cool 3 hours. Place in refrigerator after cool.

Dissolve Jello-O in one cup hot water. Add 1 package frozen strawberries. Let set until a little congealed (not too hard). Spread on cake and place back in refrigerator.

Raspberry Pecan Salad

Easy To Do Roast

Asparagus Caesar

Dome Chocolate Mousse Cake

RASPBERRY PECAN SALAD

8 cups mixed salad greens, including Boston lettuce
1 cup fresh raspberries (or strawberries)
(reserve a few to garnish salad)
1 avocado (2 if they are small)
½ lb. mushrooms, sliced
2 bunches green onions, chopped
½ cup chopped pecan

Dressing:
½ cup raspberry spreadable fruit
⅓ cup raspberry vinegar
1 T. honey
1 T. poppy seeds
1 cup canola oil

Yield: 8-10 servings

Wash greens and refrigerate until ready to serve. Combine ingredients for dressing in processor or blender. Put greens in bowl, top with remaining ingredients and toss with dressing.

EASY TO DO ROAST

Great also with brisket!

1	can cream of mushroom soup
1	package of dried onion soup mix
1	2 lb. roast

Mix the soup mix and the can of soup. Pour this mixture over the roast.

Cover well and cook slowly all day in a warm oven (250°).

This will make it's own delicious gravy.

ASPARAGUS CAESAR

2	pounds fresh asparagus
3	T. butter, melted
¼	cup lemon juice
¼	cup freshly grated Parmesan cheese
½	t. paprika

Yield: 8 servings

Snap off tough ends of asparagus: remove scales with a knife, if desired. Steam or cook asparagus, covered, in a small amount of boiling water for 6 to 8 minutes until crisp-tender; drain well.

Place asparagus in 12 × 8 × 2 baking dish. Combine butter and lemon juice; pour over asparagus. Sprinkle with cheese and paprika. Place under the broiler until browned.

"Hunger is the first course of a good dinner."

French Proverb

DOME CHOCOLATE MOUSSE CAKE

Cake:
1½ cups cake flour, sifted
1   cup unsweetened cocoa
     powder
Pinch of salt
12   eggs, separated
2   cups sugar
1   t. vanilla
¼   t. cream of tartar

Syrup:
¾   cup water
¼   cup sugar
2   T. framboise
     (raspberry eau-de-vie)

Mousse:
½   lb. bittersweet or
     semisweet chocolate
     (preferably imported),
     coarsely chopped
1   egg, beaten to blend
2   eggs, separated, room
     temperature
1   T. framboise
1   cup whipping cream

Ganache:
2   cups whipping cream
1   lb. bittersweet
     (not unsweetened) or
     semisweet chocolate
     (preferably imported),
     coarsely chopped

Raspberry Sauce:
2-10 oz. packages frozen
     sweetened raspberries,
     thawed
1   cup fresh raspberries

For cake: Preheat oven to 350°. Line 9-inch oven proof bowl or colander with foil, allowing overhang. Generously butter foil. Sift flour, cocoa powder and salt into bowl. Beat yolks and 1¾ cups sugar in another bowl until thick and pale. Blend in vanilla. Gently whisk in half of dry ingredients. Using electric mixer, beat whites and cream of tartar until soft peaks form. Add remaining ¼ cup sugar one table-spoon at a time and beat until stiff but not dry. Gently fold ⅓ of whites into batter. Fold in remaining dry ingredients, then whites. Pour into foil-lined bowl. Bake 15 minutes. Reduce oven to 325°. Continue baking until tester inserted in center comes out clean, about 50 minutes. Cool cake completely in bowl.

For syrup: Cook water and sugar in heavy small saucepan over low heat until sugar dissolves, swirling pan occasionally. Bring to boil. Cool completely. Stir in framboise.

(Continued on Next Page)

For mousse: Melt chocolate in large bowl set over pan of gently simmering water; stir until smooth. Remove bowl from over water. Whisk in egg. Whisk in yolks one at a time. Stir in framboise. Beat cream to medium, stiff peaks. Fold into chocolate mixture. Beat whites until stiff but not dry. Fold whites into melted chocolate mixture.

To assemble: Using foil overhang as handles, remove cake from bowl. Cut off 1-inch layer from flat side of cake and reserve. Return cake to bowl. Scoop out inside of cake, leaving 1-inch shell. Brush inside of cake with syrup. Fill with mousse. Brush reserved layer with syrup. Fit tightly over cake. Cover and refrigerate overnight.

For ganache: Heat cream in heavy medium saucepan. Remove from heat. Add chocolate and stir until smooth. Cool until spreadable, stirring occasionally; do not let ganache set.

For sauce: Puree thawed raspberries in processor. Strain into bowl to remove seeds. Fold in fresh raspberries.

Cream of Broccoli Soup
Oven and Grill Brisket
Southwestern Potatoes
Sautéed Green Beans
Chocolate Caramel Nut Brownies

CREAM OF BROCCOLI SOUP

2	10 oz. packages frozen chopped broccoli
¼	cup dried minced onion
3	cups chicken broth
2	T. butter
1	t. salt
⅛	t. nutmeg
2	T. flour
2	cups milk
2	cups cream
¼	t. Tabasco sauce

Yield: 8 servings

Cook broccoli and onion in chicken broth at least 5 minutes. Using blender, thoroughly blend broth and broccoli mixture until smooth. Meanwhile melt butter, add flour, salt and nutmeg. Heat until bubbly. Stir in cream, milk and Tabasco. Stir in broccoli/broth mixture and heat to serving temperature.

OVEN AND GRILL BRISKET

2	lbs. brisket
⅔	cup soy sauce
1¼	cups red cooking wine
salt and pepper (to taste)	

Yield: 4-6 servings

Place brisket in pan, salt and pepper both sides. Pour soy sauce and cooking wine over the brisket. Cook for 4 to 6 hours at 200°. Remove from oven, then cook over very slow charcoal fire for 45 minutes.

SOUTHWESTERN SCALLOPED POTATOES

4	large russet potatoes
2	medium onions
15-20	fresh mushrooms
2	cans cream of mushroom soup
1	soup can of milk

ground red pepper (to taste)
4   jalapeños, thinly sliced

Yield: 8 servings

Cut potatoes crosswise in ¼ inch slices, leaving skin on. Cut onions crosswise in ¼ inch slices and separate into rings. Slice mushrooms lengthwise in thin slices. Layer potatoes, onions and mushrooms in a 2 quart greased dish. Salt and pepper. Combine soup and milk; mix until smooth. Pour over potatoes. Sprinkle with red pepper and top with jalapenos. Bake covered at 350° for one hour. Uncover and bake 30 minutes longer. Serve immediately.

SAUTÉED GREEN BEANS

1-1¼	lbs. fresh green beans
1-3	t. oil
2-3	garlic cloves, minced
¼	t. oregano
¼	cup water
1	juice from lemon

pepper (to taste)

Yield: 8 servings

Wash fresh green beans, snap off ends. Start with 1 teaspoon of oil in skillet on low heat. Put in minced garlic and a pinch of oregano. Add green beans. Stir to coat beans. Add water, stirring occasionally, about 20 minutes or to suit taste. Before serving drizzle with fresh lemon, and sprinkle with pepper.

CHOCOLATE CARAMEL NUT BROWNIES

1	14 oz. package Kraft caramels
1	5 oz. can evaporated milk
1	package German Chocolate Cake Mix
½	cup margarine, melted
1½	cup chopped pecans
1	6 oz. package real semisweet chocolate chips

Yield: 24 servings

Heat oven to 350°. Melt caramels with ⅓ cup milk in double boiler, stirring frequently until smooth. Set aside. Mix ⅓ cup milk, cake mix and margarine in a large bowl using a wooden spoon to mix. Divide cake mixture and spread ½ in bottom of 9 x 13 inch cake pan. Press down with a spatula. Bake 8 minutes. Sprinkle chocolate chips and 1 cup nuts over hot crust. Then top with melted caramel mixture, spreading to edges of pan. Top with remaining ½ cake mixture and sprinkle with remaining nuts. Bake 18 minutes. Cool; cut into small squares and refrigerate.

FAB FIVE FOOTNOTES

Creating a fragrant home: combine 12 pieces ginger, 9 pieces stick cinnamon, 48 whole cloves, 3 t. allspice, 6 t. pickling spices. Place in jar. Simmer 3 T. of mixture in 1 quart of water in a saucepan when needed.

Coffee cans make ideal baking containers for gift breads and cakes.

Keep a food inspiration notebook in your kitchen. Use this for menus, recipe clippings, table ideas, party themes, etc...

When mixing batter, spray the beaters with non-stick spray before using and the batter won't climb up the beaters.

To remove garlic odors from your hands, rub your fingers on a silver spoon under running water.

Keep a "food" diary with menus and guests to prevent duplicating menus.

NOTES

COMIDA
MEXICANA

*Spice a dish with love and
it pleases every palate.*

Plautus

COMIDA MEXICANA

Mexican food is a basic part of our heritage as West Texans, and we never get tired of the special combination of spicy and earthy flavors that make this cuisine a southwest favorite for all casual occasions. We love to experiment with limes, avocados, green chiles, salsa, and tortillas to give these delicious ingredients a new twist. We also love the festive spirit of the cuisine and must give credit here to Stephanie for organizing the most splendid Family Fiesta night for our 12th Annual Christmas Progressive Dinner. She transformed her garage into an incredible Mexican cantina, complete with all the most delicious food we could eat. These menus are joyous presentation meals that celebrate the versatility of this homey and spirited cuisine.

Cheese Crisp
Southwestern Tortilla Soup
Mexican Shrimp Salad
Fresh Blueberry Cream Pie

CHEESE CRISP

2½	cups flour
1	cup butter
1	cup sour cream
1½	cups cheddar cheese
1½	cups mozzarella cheese
½	t. paprika

Yield: 12-15 servings

Combine the flour, butter and sour cream. Divide into four parts. Wrap each part and chill until firm. Grate 1½ cups cheddar cheese and 1½ cups mozzarella cheese. Roll out dough ¼ at a time on a well floured surface to a 12 × 6 rectangle. Sprinkle with seasoned salt. Sprinkle each rectangle with ¼ cheese mixture and roll up jelly roll style. Seal edges and ends. Sprinkle top with paprika. Bake 35 minutes at 350°. Slice.

SOUTHWESTERN TORTILLA SOUP

Delicious and easy!

Sauté in ½ cup salad oil:
½   cup chopped green chilies
½   onion, chopped
½   T. minced garlic

Add:
½   gallon tomatoes chopped
1   large can tomato juice
1   gallon water
2   T. beef base*
2   T. chicken base*
1   T. chili powder
¼   bottle A-1
¼   bottle Worcestershire
    sauce
1½   T. cumin

Toppings:
3   cups grated Monterey Jack
    Cheese
6   flour tortillas, cut
    bite-sized
2   avocados, sliced
½   cup sour cream
6   corn tortillas, crushed and
    fried

Yield: 12 servings

Simmer on low one hour. Add 3 cups grated Monterey Jack cheese and bite-sized flour tortillas. Serve with avocado slices, sour cream, crushed fried corn tortillas.

*These usually come in jars and can be found in cooking stores or gourmet section of grocery stores.

MEXICAN SHRIMP SALAD

1   lb. shrimp, cooked, diced
½   cup chopped celery
3   T. finely chopped onion
¾   cup mayonnaise
½   t. chili powder

Garnish:
lettuce leaves
tomato wedges
olives

Yield: 4 servings

In a large bowl, mix shrimp, celery, onion, mayonnaise and chili powder. Chill several hours or overnight. Serve on a bed of lettuce with tomato wedges and olives for garnish.

FRESH BLUEBERRY CREAM PIE

Quite tasty!

1	cup sour cream
2	T. flour
¾	cup sugar
1	t. vanilla extract
¼	t. salt
1	egg
2½	cups fresh blueberries
1	9-inch pastry shell, unbaked
3	T. flour
3	T. butter, softened
3	T. pecans or walnuts, chopped

Yield: 8 servings

Preheat oven to 400°. In a large bowl, combine sour cream, 2 tablespoons flour, sugar, vanilla, salt and egg. Beat 5 minutes at medium speed with an electric mixer or until smooth. Fold in blueberries. Pour filling into unbaked pastry shell. Bake for 25 minutes. In a small bowl, combine 3 tablespoons flour, butter and chopped nuts, stirring well. Sprinkle over top of pie. Bake for 10 minutes. Chill before serving.

"When men reach their sixties and retire, they go to pieces. Women just go right on cooking."

Gail Sheehy

Avocado Delights

Santa Fe Shrimp Chowder

Skillet Zucchini with Corn and Green Chiles

Enchiladas Fantastica!

Pound Cake with Mexican Chocolate Sauce

AVOCADO DELIGHTS

¾ lb. hot ground pork sausage
4 large ripe avocados, peeled and mashed
3 T. Lime juice
1 T. chopped fresh cilantro
2 T. Mayonnaise
1 cup Mexican style shredded cheese
60 small wonton wrappers
Vegetable oil

Yield: 6-8 people

Brown sausage in a large skillet over medium heat, stirring until it crumbles and is no longer pink; drain and cool. Stir together avocado, lime juice, cilantro and mayonnaise; stir in sausage and cheese. Spoon 1 Tbsp. Mixture into center of each wonton wrapper. Moisten edges with water. Fold corners of wrapper to center, enclosing filling and pinching wrapper edges to seal. Place on wax paper coated with vegetable cooking spray; cover with additional wax paper. Pour oil to a depth of 3 inches into a Dutch oven; heat to 350°. Fry wontons, 3-4 at a time, 1½ minutes on each side or until golden; drain.

SANTA FE SHRIMP AND CORN CHOWDER

¼ cup unsalted butter
2 shallots, minced
6 cups whole milk
½ cup dry, light white wine
1½ cups frozen kernels or freshly cut kernels from 3 ears of corn
2 large baking potatoes, peeled and cut into ½-inch dice
1 pound medium-size shrimp, peeled and deveined
Kosher salt and freshly ground pepper to taste
2 ripe plum tomatoes, seeded and finely diced
Chopped cilantro leaves

Yield: 4-6 servings

In a large nonreactive pot, melt the butter over medium heat. Add the shallots and cook, stirring, until softened, about 3 minutes. Add the milk, wine and corn, bring to a simmer. Do not boil. Add the potatoes and simmer until almost tender, 12-15 minutes. Add the shrimp, salt and peppper to taste, and simmer just until opaque, 3-5 minutes. Serve hot, garnishing each bowl with a handful of diced tomatoes and a sprinkle of cilantro.

SKILLET ZUCCHINI WITH CORN AND GREEN CHILIES

¼ cup butter
1 T. Olive oil
½ cup chopped onion
1-4 oz. can chopped green chilies
4 cups sliced zucchini
1½ cups fresh or frozen corn kernels
1 t. salt
¼ t. dried oregano
¼ t. cumin
½ cup chicken broth

Yield: 6 servings

Heat butter and olive oil in 12-inch skillet. Sauté onion and green chile for about 3 minutes. Add zucchini, corn, salt, oregano and cumin. Stir and mix well. Add broth. Cover skillet and simmer until zucchini is crisp-tender, about 5 minutes.

ENCHILADAS FANTASTICA!

1 lb. ground turkey or beef
2 cups picante sauce
1 10 oz. Package frozen chopped spinach, thawed, squeezed dry and chopped
2 t. ground cumin
½ t. salt
1 t. garlic powder
1 8 oz. Package regular or light cream cheese, cubed
12 (7 inch) flour tortillas, warmed
1 14 oz. can diced tomatoes in juice
1 cup cheddar cheese, shredded

Toppings:
Shredded lettuce, ripe olive slices, avocado slices, sour cream

Yield: 4-6 servings

In 10-inch nonstick skillet, cook turkey or beef until it loses its pink color and break into small pieces with a spoon. Add 1 cup picante sauce, spinach 1½ t. of the cumin and the salt. Cook and stir 5 minutes or until most of the liquid has evaporated. Add cream cheese, stirring just until melted; remove from heat. Spoon about ⅓ cup of the filling down the center of the tortilla; roll up and place seam side down in lightly greased 13 x 9 baking dish. Combine tomatoes, remaining 1 cup picante sauce and remaining ½ t. cumin; mix well. Spoon over enchiladas. Bake at 350° for 20 minutes or until hot. Sprinkle with cheddar cheese; return to oven 2 minutes to melt cheese. Top as desired and serve with additional picante sauce.

POUND CAKE WITH MEXICAN CHOCOLATE SAUCE

*For this recipe I use a store-bought pound cake
and let the wonderful flavor of the
Mexican Chocolate Sauce speak for itself!*

1	cup cocoa
½	cup sugar
¾	t. ground cinnamon
¾	cup half-and-half
½	cup butter or margarine, melted
¼	cup honey
3	T. Coffee liqueur

Yield: 6 servings

Combine first 3 ingredients in a small saucepan. Gradually whisk in half-and-half, butter and honey. Bring to a boil over medium heat, stirring constantly. Remove from heat; stir in liqueur. Serve warm over ice cream or pound cake.

Queso Dip
Sombrero Dip
Mexican Corn Soup
Camarones en Escabeche (Marinated Shrimp)
Sally's Carne Guisada
Double Apricot Margaritas

QUESO DIP
So easy and so delicious!

16 oz. Monterey Jack Cheese, shredded
2 lbs. box Velveeta Cheese
2 cans Rotel tomatoes
2 4 oz. cans chopped green chilies
1 onion, chopped
4-7 jalapeños, finely chopped
1-16 oz. jar mayonnaise
salt (to taste)
pepper (to taste)
garlic powder (to taste)

Yield: 10 servings

In microwave oven, heat Velveeta cheese until melted. Add Monterey Jack cheese. Add Rotel, chilies, onion, jalapeños, mayonnaise, salt, pepper, garlic powder and serve.

SOMBRERO DIP

1½   lbs. ground beef
½   large onion, chopped
½   bottle Heinz hot ketchup
1   can kidney beans
      (drained & mashed)
½   lb. Longhorn cheese,
      grated
1   jar Spanish olives, sliced
Garlic, to taste
Tabasco Sauce, to taste
Taco chips

Yield: 6-8 appetizer servings

Brown beef and drain. Add chopped onion, hot ketchup, kidney beans, Spanish olives, Longhorn cheese, garlic and Tabasco sauce. Heat thoroughly. Serve with taco chips.

MEXICAN CORN SOUP

3½   cups fresh or frozen corn
      kernels
1   cup chicken broth
4   T. butter
2   cups milk
1   t. ground cumin
1   clove garlic, minced
1   4 oz. can diced green
      chiles
3   dashes Tabasco sauce
1   t. ground white pepper
1   cup diced tomatoes
2   cups diced cooked
      chicken breast
1   cup shredded Peppered
      Monterey Jack cheese

Condiments:
chunky salsa
sliced black olives
sour cream
sliced green onions
diced avocados

Yield: 6-8 servings

In blender or food processor puree corn and chicken broth. Melt butter in stockpot. Add corn puree and simmer over low heat for 5 minutes, stirring constantly. Stir in milk, cumin and garlic. Heat to boiling, reduce heat and stir in green chiles, Tabasco and white pepper. Soup may be cooled and frozen at this point.

Add shredded cheese to simmering soup and stir until cheese melts. Add chicken and tomatoes. Spoon soup into bowls and garnish with condiments.

CAMARONES EN ESCABECHE (MARINATED SHRIMP)

1½   lbs. medium shrimp, cooked, peeled and deveined
⅓   cup fresh lime juice
2   medium tomatoes, chopped
1   large avocado, peeled, pitted and chopped
1   small onion, finely chopped
1   T. minced serrano chilies
2   t. minced fresh cilantro
3   T. olive oil
Salt and freshly ground black pepper to taste
Bibb lettuce
1   small red onion
Lime wedges

Yield: 6 servings

In large bowl, combine all ingredients. Refrigerate. Serve cold on a plate of Bibb lettuce and red onion rings. Garnish with lime wedges.

SALLY'S CARNE GUISADA

Ask your butcher to cut this steak.

4-7 lb. 7-bone steak (thick)
2-4 T. cooking oil
2   tomatoes, diced
1   medium onion, diced
½   t. garlic powder
½   t. cumin powder
½   cup salsa

Yield: 8-10 servings

Cut meat into bite-sized pieces. Cook meat in oil until tender. Add tomatoes and onions; cook until onion is tender. Add rest of ingredients. Salt to taste; simmer low heat for 30 minutes.

Serve on a bed of brown rice.

DOUBLE APRICOT MARGARITAS

1 ¼   cup halved, pitted and
      unpeeled apricots,
      or one 16 oz. can
      unpeeled apricot halves
      (juice packed), drained
½   cup tequila
¼   cup sugar
¼   cup lime juice
¼   cup apricot nectar
20-24 ice cubes

Yield: 8-10 servings

Blend all ingredients, then add ice. Blend until slushy, rub lime juice on the rim of the glass and dip in salt.

Sour Cream Guacamole and Chips
Lisa's Tortilla Soup
Mexican Rice
Green Chicken Enchiladas
Lime Meringue Pie with Coconut Crust

SOUR CREAM GUACAMOLE

3   medium avocados (pretty soft)
1   T. sour cream
1   t. freshly squeezed lemon juice
1   T. fresh garlic
1   tomato, peeled, seeded and finely chopped
Salt, to taste

Yield: 4 servings

Mash avocados; mix in other ingredients. Add tomatoes for garnish. Serve with chips.

"No mean woman can cook well, for it calls for a light head, a generous spirit and a large heart."

Paul Gauguin

LISA'S TORTILLA SOUP

This recipe comes from my sister who makes it during Christmas. . . a great change from the traditional Turkey!

1 can cream of chicken soup
4 chicken breasts, cooked and diced
6 green onions, chopped
3 medium tomatoes, peeled
3 ribs celery, chopped
1 T. chopped green chilies
½ bell pepper, chopped
2 T. vegetable oil
6 corn tortillas, halved and sliced in ¼" strips
Vegetable Oil
4½ cup chicken broth
1 bay leaf, crushed
½ t. coriander
salt & pepper to taste

Topping:
cheddar cheese, grated, avocado, sliced

Yield: 8 servings

Sauté onions, tomatoes, celery, green chilies and bell pepper in the 2 T. oil until soft. Remove with a slotted spoon and set aside. Fry tortilla strips in more oil until crisp. Drain on a paper towel. Bring broth to a boil and add veggies, tortilla strips, bay leaf, coriander, cream of chicken soup and chicken breasts. Simmer, covered 30 minutes. Add salt, pepper. Serve with grated cheese and avocado.

MEXICAN RICE

1 cup uncooked rice
1 T. butter (or oil)
cumin (to taste)
oregano (to taste)
garlic salt (to taste)
onion salt (to taste)
½ can stewed tomatoes
1 small green pepper, finely chopped

Yield: 4 servings

Brown the rice in the oil. Add all of the spices and then the stewed tomatoes with a little of the juice. Stir in the green pepper. Heat thoroughly.

115

GREEN CHICKEN ENCHILADAS (OR BEEF)

2	pounds beef or 4 chicken breasts (cooked & cubed)
1	small onion (chopped)
2-3	t. garlic powder

salt and pepper (to taste)

1	pound Velveeta cheese
1	can evaporated milk
1	can cream of chicken soup
1	can cream of mushroom soup
1	small can chopped chilies
25	tortillas
½	cup vegetable oil
1-1½	cups grated Monterey Jack cheese

Yield: 20-25 enchiladas.

Brown the meat and add the onion, garlic powder, salt and pepper. Next melt together the Velveeta cheese, evaporated milk, both soups and the chilies. Soften tortillas by heating them in the hot oil. Add a spoonful of the meat mixture and a small amount of grated Monterey Jack cheese on each tortilla. Roll up tight as possible and place in a casserole dish. Repeat with each tortilla. Pour cheese mixture over enchiladas. Bake at 350° until bubbly.

Friendship in Tough Times

Plato advised; "Be kind for everyone you meet is fighting a hard battle." He might have added that sometimes the battle rages so fiercely that we must call in the reserves. Trusted friends are the reserve troops who help us survive and conquer the inevitable skirmishes of life.

LIME MERINGUE PIE WITH COCONUT CRUST

Very good with Mexican food.

Crust:
1	cup lightly packed grated coconut
¾	cup fine dry bread crumbs
2	T. sugar
3	T. unsalted butter, melted

Filling:
¾	cup sugar
5	T. cornstarch
1	T. unbleached white flour
1	cup heavy whipping cream
1	cup half-and-half
3	extra large egg yolks
½	cup fresh lime juice

Finely grated zest of 1 lime

Meringue:
4	extra large egg whites
3	T. sugar

Pinch of cream of tartar
1-2 T. grated coconut for garnish (optional)

Yield: 8-10 servings

Preheat the oven to 350°. Mix the coconut, bread crumbs, 2 tablespoons sugar, and butter in a bowl or in a food processor until blended. Pat the mixture into a 9 inch pie plate, evenly covering the bottom and sides. Bake for 15 minutes or until the crust is pale golden brown. Cool on a baking rack.

To prepare the filling, mix the sugar, cornstarch, and flour in a heavy saucepan. Add the creams, whisking them in until well blended. Place the pan over medium-low heat and cook for 8 to 10 minutes, stirring regularly, until the mixture is slightly thickened.

Beat the egg yolks well in a bowl. Add a little of the cream mixture to the eggs, blending well. Add a bit more cream and blend well. Carefully add the egg and cream mixture to the saucepan. Cook over low heat for about 2 minutes; do not allow the mixture to boil. Remove from the heat, stir in the lime juice and zest, cover with wax paper, and let cool to room temperature.

Preheat the oven to 400°. Pour the filling into the crust. To prepare the meringue, beat the whites in a bowl until foamy. Add the sugar and cream of tartar end beat the whites until stiff but not dry. Mound the whites onto the filling and spread them evenly, taking care to make sure the whites touch the entire perimeter of the crust.

Sprinkle the meringue with the extra coconut, if desired. Bake the pie for 5 minutes, or until the meringue is lightly browned. Let cool on a wire rack and then refrigerate 2 to 3 hours before serving.

Debbie's Salsa and Tortilla Chips
Green Chili Enchiladas
Refried Beans
Baked Spicy Corn
Lime Angel Pie
Frozen Margarita Punch

DEBBIE'S SALSA

1 pound can whole tomatoes
2 fresh jalapeños (seeded)
2 bunches green onions
garlic (to taste)
tortilla chips

Yield: 4 servings

Put all ingredients in a blender and pulse to chop. Add garlic salt to taste. Serve with tortilla chips.

GREEN CHILI ENCHILADAS

Delicious!

1 pound ground meat
1 small onion, chopped
8 oz. longhorn cheese, grated
1 can cream of chicken soup
1 small can chopped green chilies
1 small jar chopped pimientos
1 small can evaporated milk
8 oz. Velveeta cheese
10-15 corn tortillas
Vegetable oil

Yield: 10-15 enchiladas

Brown the ground meat with the onion. Add the longhorn cheese and simmer. In a double boiler mix the soup, chilies, pimientos, evaporated milk and the Velveeta cheese until the cheese is melted and all is mixed together.

Soften tortillas in hot oil. Roll meat mixture in tortillas. Place in pan and pour green chili mixture over enchiladas. Cover with foil and bake at 400° until mixture is bubbly.

REFRIED BEANS

¼ cup vegetable oil or
  bacon drippings
4 cups cooked pinto beans
1 cup grated Monterey Jack
  or American cheese
  (optional)

Yield: 8 servings

Heat oil or drippings in a heavy
skillet until smoking hot. Carefully
add 1 cup of the cooked beans for
1 minute, mashing as you stir. Add
the remaining beans, turn the heat
to low, and continue mashing the
beans until smooth and creamy
(cook for about 10 to 15 minutes).
Sprinkle with cheese if desired and
allow to melt before serving.

BAKED SPICY CORN

2 eggs
½ cup whole milk
1 (14 oz.) can corn kernels
1 (14 oz.) can creamed corn
½ cup cornmeal
1 T. flour
1 t. salt
3 cups grated American
  cheese
1 t. black pepper
¼ cup bacon drippings,
  vegetable oil, or butter
¼ cup chopped pickled
  jalapeños, optional

Yield: 12-15 servings

Preheat the oven to 350°. In a
bowl, thoroughly beat the eggs
and combine them with the milk.
Pour the mixture into a 12 × 14
inch baking dish. Mix all the
remaining ingredients, including
the jalapeños (if desired) and add
to baking pan.

Bake for 45 to 50 minutes, until
the ingredients are firm and set
up.

LIME ANGEL PIE

Light and luscious.

Meringue Crust:

4   egg whites, room
     temperature
¼   t. cream of tartar
1   cup sugar

Filling:

4   egg yolks
⅛   t. salt
½   cup sugar
¼   cup, fresh lime juice
1   T. grated lime peel
½   pint whipping cream
green food coloring
½   pint whipping cream
1   lime, sliced thinly

Yield: 8 servings

Preheat oven to 275°. Grease a 9½ or 10 inch pie plate; set aside. In a large bowl, beat egg whites and cream of tartar until soft peaks form. Gradually add sugar 1 tablespoon at a time, beating until very stiff. Spoon the meringue into prepared pie plate, mounding the sides up and over the edge. Bake one hour. Remove from oven and cool.

Beat egg yolks and salt in a medium bowl until light and fluffy. Stir in sugar, lime juice and peel. Place mixture in the top of a double boiler over boiling water. Stir constantly, until thickened and smooth, 8-10 minutes. Remove from heat. Cool. Beat ½ pint cream until stiff. Fold into lime mixture and add a dash of food coloring. Pour into meringue crust. Chill. Before serving, garnish or cover with additional whipped cream and lime slices.

FROZEN MARGARITA PUNCH

4   12 oz. cans frozen
     limeade concentrate,
     undiluted
3   quarts water
3   cups orange liqueur
3   cups tequila
2   2 liter bottles of Sprite,
     chilled
sliced limes for garnish

Yield: 2½ gallons

Combine first 4 ingredients in a large bowl. Pour mixture into plastic freezer bags and freeze at least 8 hours. Remove from the freezer 10 minutes before serving. Break into pieces and place in pitcher or punch bowl. Add Sprite and stir until slushy. Serve immediately.

FAB FIVE FOOT NOTES

If using nacho chips or nuts in a recipe, improve their flavor by placing them in the oven at a low temperature until they have been warmed.

Green avocados? Place in a drawer with dishtowels. Check each day until they are ripe.

To freshen stale tortilla chips, put them in a paper bag and microwave at 10-second intervals until crispy.

To quickly de-seed a avocado, slice avocado lengthwise into halves; separate halves. Firmly hit seed with knife; pit should stick into knife. Quickly twist knife and remove seed.

Peel cloves of garlic and keep in a jar filled with vegetable or olive oil in refrigerator. Will keep indefinitely and the garlic-flavored oil makes a wonderful base for salad dressing.

NOTES

SUMMER
BARBECUES

*"Summer cooking implies a sense of immediacy,
a capacity to capture the essence
of the fleeting moment."*
Elizabeth David

SUMMER BARBECUES

What began as another way for us to get together with our husbands and children for a night of great food and fun, has evolved into one more weekend event alternating between Lubbock and Fort Worth. The men golf, the women shop, and the seven children draw a magic circle around their own activities. In between all the events, of course, we cook, and our husbands join in to prepare the great grilled tastes of lazy summer. These menus and recipes are from our fun-filled summer weekends together.

Spicy Guacamole
Sun Dried Tomato Spread
Okra Rellenos
Couscous Salad with
Apricots, Pine Nuts and Ginger
Mixed Grill
Roasted Garlic Potatoes
Lemon Blueberry Cream Pie

SPICY GUACAMOLE

4-5 avocados
1   jar Old El Paso Thick and
     Chunky Salsa
1   T. lemon juice

Yield: 4 servings

Mash avocados and stir in salsa
and lemon juice. Serve with
chips.

SUN-DRIED TOMATO SPREAD

1-2 cloves garlic, minced
1 T. olive oil
1/3 cup dry white wine
1/2 cup dried tomatoes, snipped
1 8 oz. package cream cheese, softened
1/3 cup snipped fresh basil
3 T. grated Parmesan cheese
Baguette-style French bread slices, toasted
Fresh basil (optional)

Yield: 1 cup

In a medium skillet cook garlic in oil until light brown. Add wine and dried tomatoes. Cook, uncovered, over low heat for 15 minutes. Remove from heat; let stand 10 minutes. Drain excess liquid. Meanwhile, in a food processor bowl or blender container combine cream cheese, snipped basil, and Parmesan cheese. Cover and process or blend until smooth. Transfer to serving bowl. Cover and chill 4 to 24 hours. Let stand at room temperature 30 minutes before serving. Serve with toasted baguette slices. Garnish with fresh basil, if desired.

OKRA RELLENOS

A Great Texas snack.

4 oz. Monterey Jack cheese with peppers
1 lb. fresh okra (4-inch-long pods)
1 cup self-rising flour
1/3 cup self-rising cornmeal
1 large egg
1/2 cup buttermilk
1/2 cup dark beer
corn oil
1/2 t. salt
Salsa

Yield: 2 dozen

Cut Monterey Jack cheese into 3 × 1/4 × 1/4 inch sticks. Cut a lengthwise slit in each okra pod, cutting to but not through ends; push seeds aside. Stuff pods with cheese sticks, and set aside.

Combine flour and cornmeal in a large bowl; make a well in center of mixture. Stir together egg, buttermilk, and beer; add to dry ingredients, stirring until smooth.

Pour oil to depth of 3 inches into a Dutch oven; heat to 375°. Dip stuffed okra in batter, coating well; fry, a few at a time, in hot oil until golden. Drain on paper towels. Sprinkle with salt; serve immediately with salsa.

COUSCOUS SALAD WITH APRICOTS, PINE NUTS AND GINGER

Nice and unusual summer salad.

1	cup instant couscous
½	cup water
1	cup fresh orange juice
¼	cup light olive oil
2½	T. Champagne vinegar
8	dried apricots, thinly sliced (about ⅓ cup)
1	T. dried currants
1	T. golden raisins
2	t. grated fresh ginger
½	t. Salt
½	cup finely diced red onion
2	T. pine nuts, toasted

Yield: 4-6 servings

Pour the couscous into a small mixing bowl. Combine water, orange juice, oil, and two table-spoons vinegar in a medium-size saucepan. Bring the liquid just to a boil and stir in the dried fruit, ginger, and ½ teaspoon salt; pour immediately over the couscous. Cover the bowl and let it sit for 20 minutes.

Bring a small pot of water to a boil and drop in the red onion for 15 seconds. Drain well; toss the onion with a few splashes of vinegar to draw out its pink color.

Fluff the couscous with a fork and toss with pine nuts and onion. Add salt to season and an additional splash of vinegar to brighten the flavor.

It is great to have friends when one is young,
but indeed it is still more so when you are getting old.
When we are young, friends are,
like everything else, a matter of course.
In the old days, we know what it means to have them.

Edvard Grieg

MIXED GRILL

2   T. soy sauce
1   T. minced fresh ginger
1   T. lemon zest
2   t. Asian sesame oil
1   clove garlic, minced
1   t. coarsely ground black
     pepper
1   t. brown sugar
1   flank steak (about 1½
     pounds)
2   pounds hot Italian
     sausage, in 2 coils
Olive oil

Yield: 6 servings

In a shallow bowl large enough to hold the steak, stir the marinade ingredients together. Add the steak, and turn it in the marinade; rub marinade into the surface. Cover loosely, and refrigerate overnight. Prepare hot coals for grilling. Pierce each sausage coil with two skewers at right angles, to hold the shape and facilitate turning. Brush the sausages well with olive oil. Grill the sausages over high heat until cooked through and lightly charred, about 7 minutes per side. Set aside, loosely covered with aluminum foil. Remove the steak from the marinade, and grill it over high heat, 4-5 minutes per side. Slice the steak thinly on the diagonal, and cut the sausages into large chunks. Serve immediately.

ROASTED GARLIC POTATOES

¾   pound red potatoes
6   large garlic cloves
     (unpeeled), flattened
1   T. olive oil
2   t. dried rosemary,
     crumbled
Salt and freshly ground pepper

Yield: 4 servings

Preheat oven to 450°. Cut potatoes into 1¼ inch wide wedges. Combine potatoes, garlic, oil and rosemary in 8 inch square baking dish. Season generously with salt and pepper. Roast until potatoes are tender and crusty, stirring occasionally, about 45 minutes.

LEMON-BLUEBERRY CREAM PIE

1	cup sugar
3	T. Cornstarch
1	cup milk
3	egg yolks, beaten
¼	cup butter or margarine
1	T. finely shredded lemon peel
¼	cup lemon juice
1	8 oz. carton sour cream
2	cups fresh blueberries
1	9 inch baked pastry shell

Sweetened whipped cream (optional)
Lemon slices (optional)

Yield: 8 servings

In a saucepan combine 1 cup sugar and cornstarch. Add milk, egg yolks, butter, and 1 T. lemon peel. Cook and stir over medium heat until thickened and bubbly; cook and stir 2 minutes more. Remove from heat; stir in lemon juice. Transfer to a bowl; cover surface with plastic wrap and refrigerate till cool. When cool; stir sour cream and blueberries into mixture; pour into pastry shell. Cover and chill at least 4 hours. If desired, stir a little lemon peel into sweetened whipped cream. Pipe or spoon atop pie. Garnish with lemon slices, if desired.

Ovid observed, "As the yellow gold is tried in fire,
so the faith of friendship must be seen in adversity."
If you have an acquaintance who is being tested by fire,
volunteer your services today. Who knows?
Your support might just turn the tide of battle.

Summer Salad
Steph's Pinto Beans
Hash Brown Potato Casserole
Steph's Famous Brisket
Chocolate Sheath Cake

A McKee family menu favorite.

SUMMER SALAD

There is nothing better than summer tomatoes, cucumbers, and peppers at the peak of their season. This simple salad combines the three with an oil free, old-fashioned dressing.

4	medium sized tomatoes
2	large cucumbers
1	small sweet green pepper
1	small sweet red pepper
1	small jalapeño pepper (optional but adds lots of flavor)—grate it for a more subtle flavor (use gloves!)

Vinegar-and-sugar dressing

Yield: 8-10 servings

In large bowl, combine all ingredients and dressing. Toss; cover and refrigerate until ready to serve.

Vinegar and Sugar Dressing:

½	cup cider vinegar
3	T. sugar
¼	t. salt
¼	t. pepper

Cover tightly and shake well.

STEPH'S PINTO BEANS

32 oz. bag of pinto beans
3 qts. water
2-3 T. chili powder
Salt and pepper to taste

Yield: 8 Servings

Sort and wash beans before cooking. Bring water to a rapid boil. Slowly stir in beans. Reduce heat, boil gently until beans are tender; 2-2½ hours. Add salt, pepper and chili powder last ½ hour of cooking. Watch the water level in the beans as they cook and add hot water as needed.

HASH BROWN POTATO CASSEROLE

This is a big favorite in our families.
Make one and freeze one.

1 (32 oz.) package shredded or country style frozen hash brown potatoes
1 cup butter melted and halved
1 can cream of chicken soup
12 oz. cheddar cheese, grated
1 cup sour cream
1 t. salt
½ small onion chopped
1½ cups corn flakes

Yield: 12-15 servings.

Place thawed potatoes in 9 × 13 casserole. Mix ½ cup butter, soup, cheese, sour cream, salt and onion over low heat. Pour over potatoes. Top with corn flakes, mixed with ½ cup butter. Bake uncovered at 350° for 45 minutes.

(Especially good buffet dish!) Freezes well too.

"A picnic is a state of mind and can be made anywhere."

Anonymous

STEPH'S BRISKET

Well trimmed Brisket—size according to your crowd, but remember they do shrink when they cook.

6-8 lbs. well trimmed Brisket
3 T. Liquid Smoke
3 T. Worcestershire sauce
1 large onion, sliced
1 T. course ground pepper
1 cup water

Yield: 8 servings

Place brisket in a roasting pan. Add 1 cup water. Pour liquid smoke and worcestershire sauce over the brisket. Shake pepper over the meat and cover the brisket with sliced onion. The secret to this is cooking it slow all day. 275° for 7-8 hours.

CHOCOLATE SHEATH CAKE

Combine in large bowl:
2 cups sugar
2 cups flour

Bring to a rapid boil the following:

1 stick butter
½ cup Crisco
4 T. cocoa
1 cup water

Pour this over sugar and flour. Add:

½ cup buttermilk
1 t. soda
pinch salt
2 eggs
1 t. vanilla

Bake in 9 x 13 pan at 400° for 20 minutes.

Icing:
1 stick butter
4 T. cocoa
½ cup coffee

Bring to a boil and pour over one box of powdered sugar. Let cool and ice cake.

Fiesta Dip

Venezuelan Brisket

Red and Yellow Pepper Salad

Potato Chip Cookies

Chocolate Chip Cookie Sticks

FIESTA DIP

Always the "hit" at a party.

2	pounds Monterey Jack cheese, shredded
4	oz. can olives, sliced
4	oz. can green chilies, chopped
1	bunch green onion, chopped
4	tomatoes, chopped

1   8 oz. bottle Italian Dressing
¼   cup parsley, chopped
¼   cup cilantro, chopped

Yield: 12-15 appetizer servings

Mix all together and enjoy with crackers or chips.

VENEZUELAN BRISKET

6   lbs. brisket
3   T. oil
Water
1   onion, chopped
1   green bell pepper, chopped
3   tomatoes, chopped
Salt & pepper to taste
1   T. garlic salt

Put oil in Dutch oven; enough to coat brisket. Add one inch water. Cover and cook over medium-high heat until brisket is soft (about 1½ hours).

Sauté onion, pepper and tomatoes until clear. Add meat juice. Season with salt, pepper and garlic salt. Shred cooked brisket. Add to the juice; heat.

RED AND YELLOW PEPPER SALAD

1   large red onion, thinly sliced and separated into rings
1   T. balsamic or red wine vinegar
2   medium-size red bell peppers, stemmed, seeded, and cut into strips
1   medium-size yellow bell pepper, stemmed, seeded, and finely diced
2   medium-size cucumbers, thinly sliced

Yield: 8 servings

Tarragon Vinaigrette (recipe follows)

In a wide frying pan, combine onion and vinegar. Cook over medium heat, stirring, for 2 minutes. Let cool.

In a large bowl, combine onion mixture, red and yellow bell peppers, and cucumbers. Prepare Tarragon Vinaigrette. Pour over vegetables and toss well. If made ahead, cover and refrigerate until next day, stirring several times.

Tarragon Vinaigrette: Mix ½ cup white wine vinegar, 1 tablespoon olive oil or salad oil, 2 teaspoons sugar, 1 teaspoon dry tarragon leaves; 1 clove garlic minced or pressed, and ¼ teaspoon pepper.

POTATO CHIP COOKIES

Sounds a little strange, but you will love them.
They are one of our all time favorites.

1   cup butter, softened
½   cup sugar
1   t. vanilla
1½   cups sifted flour
¾   cup crushed potato chips*
½   cup chopped pecans
sifted powdered sugar

Yield: 3-5 dozen

Cream butter and sugar. Add vanilla, flour, chips and nuts. Drop on ungreased cookie sheets. Bake 15 to 18 minutes at 325°. After baking, shake on powdered sugar with sifter.

Very fragile!

*Use only salted, smooth potato chips. No BBQ, Ruffles, Pringles, etc.

CHOCOLATE CHIP
COOKIE STICKS

½	cup shortening
½	cup butter, softened
1	cup packed brown sugar
½	cup granulated sugar
½	t. baking soda
2	eggs
2	t. vanilla
2½	cups all-purpose flour
8	oz. semisweet chocolate, coarsely chopped
1	cup chopped walnuts, pecans or hazelnuts

Yield: 18 long cookies

Preheat oven to 375°. In large mixing bowl beat the shortening and butter with an electric mixer on medium to high speed for 30 seconds. Add the brown sugar, granulated sugar, and baking soda. Beat mixture until combined, scraping the sides of the bowl occasionally. Beat in the eggs and vanilla until combined. Beat in as much of the flour as you can with the mixer. With a wooden spoon stir in remaining flour. Stir in chocolate and if desired, nuts.

Press dough evenly into a foil lined 13 x 9 x 2 inch baking pan. Bake for 22 to 25 minutes or until golden brown and center is set.

Cool in pan for 1 hour on a wire rack. Preheat oven to 325°. Holding securely to foil lining, gently remove cookies from pan and place on a cutting board, leaving cookies on foil lining. Cut crosswise into 9 x ½ inch slices. Places slices, cut side down about 1 inch apart on ungreased cookie sheet. Bake for 6 to 8 minutes or until cut edges are crispy. Carefully transfer cookies to wire rack. (cookies will be tender) Cool.

Black-Eyed Pea Dip

Marinated Beef Brisket

Grilled Vegetables with Tomato-Basil Sauce

Baked Acorn Squash with sautéed Spinach and Pinenuts

Cornbread Casserole

Sweet Summer Pie

BLACK-EYED PEA DIP

Sooo good!

2	15 oz. cans black-eyed peas, drained
1½	cups Monterey Jack cheese with jalapeños, shredded
½	cup green onion, chopped
½	small onion, chopped
1	garlic clove, minced
½	cup butter
1	4 oz. can green chilies, drained

Yield: 8 appetizer servings

Preheat oven to 350°. Blend all ingredients in food processor just until mixed. Pour into greased baking dish and bake for 20 minutes. Serve hot or cold with chips or vegetables.

136

MARINADE FOR BRISKET (OR PORK TENDERLOINS)

½   cup teriyaki sauce
½   cup soy sauce
3   T. brown sugar
2   green onions, chopped
1   clove garlic, pressed
1   T. sesame seeds
½   t. ground ginger
½   t. pepper
1   T. vegetable oil
4-5 lb. brisket (or pork tenderloin)

Combine first 9 ingredients in a shallow dish. Add meat and turn to coat. Cover and refrigerate 2-4 hours. Cook meat, covered, over medium hot coals for 20 minutes, turn once.

GRILLED VEGETABLES WITH TOMATO-BASIL SAUCE

4   fennel bulbs, trimmed and cut in half
or
2   lbs. mushrooms
or
4   medium-sized red onions, peeled and cut in ½ pieces
1/3 cup olive oil
¼   cup minced onions
2   large cloves garlic, chopped
5   large ripe roma tomatoes, seeded and diced
1   T. lemon juice
2   T. chopped basil
salt and pepper to taste

Yield: 6 servings

Prepare grill. Brush vegetables generously with salt and pepper. Place vegetables on grill and cook 3 to 5 minutes on each side of the fennel, about 5 minutes on mushrooms and about 2 to 3 minutes for each side of onion. Remove from grill and keep warm until served.

In a skillet heat 2 tablespoons of olive oil and sauté minced onions until transparent. Add garlic and cook about 30 seconds. Stir in roma tomatoes and lemon juice. Cook about 3 minutes. Remove from the stove and stir in basil and season with salt and pepper.

BAKED ACORN SQUASH WITH SAUTÉED SPINACH AND PINE NUTS

2 medium acorn squash
1 T. butter, melted
salt and pepper
4 slices bacon
1 lb. fresh spinach
¼ cup raisins
½ cup grated parmesan cheese
½ cup pine nuts
½ cup buttered bread crumbs

Yield: 4 servings

Preheat oven to 375°. Cut the squash in half and remove the seeds. Brush all cut surfaces with melted butter. Sprinkle with salt and pepper. Cover with foil and bake cut side up for 35 minutes or until tender. Meanwhile, dice bacon and fry until just crisp. Remove from pan and set aside.

Wash spinach well and spin dry. Sauté the spinach with the raisins in the bacon drippings until spinach is wilted and dark green. Stir in parmesan cheese and pine nuts. Spoon mixture into each of the four squash halves. Sprinkle tops with buttered bread crumbs and return to oven until crumbs are golden brown.

CORNBREAD CASSEROLE

8½ ounce package corn bread mix
2 eggs
1 (8 oz.) can cream corn
1 (8 oz.) can whole kernel corn, drained
½ cup sour cream
1 stick butter or margarine

Yield: 4-6 servings

Preheat oven to 375°. Melt butter in 8 x 8 x 2 baking pan. Combine remaining ingredients and pour into dish. Bake for 40 minutes.

SWEET SUMMER PIE

Best during summer months when fruit is in season.

1	9 inch refrigerated piecrust
1	large orange
1	medium lemon
4	large eggs, separated
1/3	cup sugar and 1/4 cup sugar
1/3	cup all-purpose flour
8	medium nectarines (or frozen peaches—about 2½ lbs.)
1/2	pint raspberries

Yield: 10 servings

Early in day:

Let piecrust stand at room temperature as label directs.

Meanwhile, from orange, grate 2 t. peel and squeeze 1/3 cup juice. From lemon, grate 1½ t. peel and squeeze enough juice to add to orange juice to equal ½ cup juice in total.

In small bowl, with mixer at high speed, beat egg yolks, salt, and 1/3 cup sugar until thick and lemon-colored, about 3 minutes. Gradually beat in juice and peels. In 1 quart saucepan over low heat, cook yolk mixture until thick, 8 to 10 minutes, stirring constantly (do not boil or mixture will curdle). Spoon into medium bowl; cool.

Preheat oven to 425°. In large bowl, mix flour and 1/3 cup sugar. Peel, pit and slice nectarines; toss with flour mixture; gently stir in raspberries.

Line 9 inch pie plate with piecrust as label directs. Spoon in nectarine mixture. Cover pie loosely with lightly greased foil; bake 45 minutes or until fruit mixture is hot and bubbly and crust is lightly browned.

Remove pie from oven. Reduce oven temperature to 350°. In small bowl, with mixer at high speed, beat egg whites to soft peaks. Sprinkle in 1/4 cup sugar, beating until whites stand in stiff peaks. Fold egg white mixture into yolk mixture, one-third at a time.

Spread soufflé topping over filling. Return pie to oven; bake 15 minutes or until soufflé is set and top is browned. Cool pie on wire rack at least 3 hours. Cover and refrigerate any leftovers.

Seafood Cocktail Spread
Southern Hash Brown Casserole
Corn and Black Bean Salad
Grilled Steaks with Garlic Steak Butter
Buttermilk Fudge Squares

SEAFOOD COCKTAIL SPREAD

1   10¾ oz. can cream of mushroom soup or cream of celery soup
2   ¼ oz. envelopes unflavored gelatin (we recommend Knox)
3   T. water
1   cup mayonnaise
1   8 oz. package cream cheese, softened
1   cup finely chopped celery
1   small onion, finely chopped
14 oz. cooked, flaked crabmeat
14 oz. cooked shrimp, chopped

Yield: 2 quarts

In saucepan, heat mushroom soup adding gelatin and water. Bring to boil. Set aside and let cool completely. In a large bowl, mix mayonnaise and cream cheese. Stir in celery, onion, crabmeat and shrimp. To the seafood mixture, add mushroom soup and stir thoroughly. In a 2 quart mold or fish-shaped mold, pour seafood mixture. Chill until firm. Serve with fancy crackers.

"In cooking as in all the arts, simplicity is the sign of perfection."

Aurnousky

SOUTHERN HASH BROWN CASSEROLE

1	2 lb. package frozen hash brown potatoes, thawed
½	cup melted butter or oleo
½	t. black pepper
2	t. salt
¼	t. cumin
½	cup chopped onion
1	can cream of chicken soup
1	cup sour cream
1	cup half & half
10	oz. cheddar cheese, grated

Yield: 12-15 servings

Mix all ingredients together and bake in a 13 × 9 baking dish for 1½ to 2 hours at 325°.

CORN AND BLACK BEAN SALAD

Yummy Salad!

4	cups fresh or frozen corn kernels
2	15 oz. can black beans, drained and rinsed
3	medium size tomatoes, seeded and chopped
¼	cup minced cilantro
½	cup minced red onion

Cumin dressing (recipe follows)

In a 4 to 5 quart pan, bring 2 quarts water to a boil over high heat. Add corn and cook until tender (about 5 minutes). Drain, rinse with cold water until cool, and drain again. In a salad bowl, stir together corn, beans, tomatoes, cilantro and onion. Prepare Cumin Dressing. Pour over vegetables and toss well. If made ahead, cover and refrigerate until next day.

Cumin Dressing:

¼	cup lime juice
⅓	cup sherry vinegar (or red wine vinegar)
1	T. Dijon mustard
2	t. ground cumin
4	T. salad oil

Yield: 10 servings

Stir together lime juice, sherry vinegar, Dijon mustard and cumin. Add oil and whisk until blended.

141

GRILLED STEAKS WITH GARLIC STEAK BUTTER

1 ½ inch thick steak
      (your choice)
lemon pepper (to taste)
garlic powder (to taste)
seasoned salt (to taste)
Garlic Steak Butter (recipe
      follows)

Have steaks cut an inch and a half thick. If possible, allow them to reach room temperature before cooking. About 15 minutes prior to cooking, season both sides with lemon pepper, quite a bit of garlic powder, and seasoned salt.

Cook over a **HOT** charcoal fire, about **10 TO 12 INCHES FROM THE MEAT**, for 7½ to 8 minutes per side for medium rare, **TURNING ONLY ONCE.** If you want them more done, you should cook them for about 5 minutes per side and then turn them every 2 or 3 minutes until they reach the desired doneness. Cooking times will need to be adjusted for thinner or thicker steaks. With a charcoal fire, don't put the steaks on until the coals are completely gray.

GARLIC STEAK BUTTER

½   lb. butter
1   T. Cavenders Seasoning
½   t. chopped parsley
1   t. chopped garlic

Allow the butter to soften at room temperature. Combine all ingredients and cream together. Spread on steaks immediately after grilling.

BUTTERMILK FUDGE SQUARES

Similar to chocolate sheet cake but thinner.

1 cup butter
¼ cup cocoa
1 cup water
½ cup buttermilk
2 large eggs
1 t. baking soda
1 t. vanilla extract
2 cups sugar
2 cups all-purpose flour
½ t. salt
Chocolate-Buttermilk Frosting
   (Recipe follows)

Yield: 2 dozen

Cook first 3 ingredients in a small saucepan over low heat, stirring constantly, until butter melts and mixture is smooth; remove from heat.

Beat buttermilk and next 3 ingredients at medium speed with an electric mixer until smooth. Add butter mixture to buttermilk mixture, beating until blended.

Combine sugar, flour and salt; gradually add to buttermilk mixture, beating until blended. Pour into a greased 15 x 10 inch jellyroll pan.

Bake cake at 350° for 15 to 20 minutes or until set. Spread Chocolate-Buttermilk Frosting over warm cake. Cut into squares while warm. Cool before serving.

Chocolate-Buttermilk Frosting:

1 cup butter
¼ cup cocoa
1/3 cup buttermilk
1 (16 oz.) package
   powdered sugar
1 t. vanilla extract
¼ cup chopped pecans

Yield: about 2½ cups

Cook first 3 ingredients in a medium saucepan over medium heat, stirring constantly, until butter melts and mixture is smooth. Remove from heat; stir in powdered sugar, vanilla and pecans.

Phyl's Favorite Salad
Lemon Roasted Chicken
Vegetable Rice Medley
Homemade Vanilla (or Peach) Ice Cream

PHYL'S FAVORITE SALAD
Love the variety of this salad.

1	head of lettuce (any type)
1	bunch green onions, chopped
½	lb. mushrooms, sliced
½	cup Feta cheese
½	cup walnuts, chopped
1	large garlic bud (roast until charred but not burned)
1	large or 2 small red or green peppers (roast until charred but not burned)

Optional:

4	oz. jar marinated artichoke hearts
1	cup grapes (halved)
2	oz. snow peas
2	oz. dried green peas
¼	cup pumpkin or sunflower seeds

Yield: 6-8 servings

Dressing (mix the following together):

⅓	cup balsamic vinegar
½	cup olive oil
½	cup mayonnaise
½	cup sugar
1	t. pepper
1	t. garlic salt
1	t. of any kind of green flaky spices

(i.e.: parsley, cilantro, but NOT oregano)

Put in a jar and shake until mixed. Refrigerate until ready to serve, then toss with the greens and other ingredients.

LEMON ROASTED CHICKEN

How easy is this!

2	garlic bulbs, minced
1	cup fresh lemon juice
1½	t. pepper
1	T. salt
⅔	cup fresh rosemary
2	cup olive oil
3	chickens, cut in pieces
3	lemons, sliced

Yield: 12-15 servings

Whisk together first 5 ingredients until blended, whisk in olive oil.

Pour mixture evenly into 3 large heavy-duty zip-top plastic bags; add chicken pieces and lemon slices. Seal and chill 8 hours, turning bags occasionally.

Line 2 (10 x 15) jellyroll pans with aluminum foil. Remove chicken pieces from marinade and arrange in pans. Drizzle with marinade.

Bake at 425° for 1 hour or until done, basting with pan juices every 20 minutes.

VEGETABLE RICE MEDLEY

1	cup uncooked long grain rice
2¼	cups water
2-3	T. onion or vegetable soup mix
¼	t. salt
2	cups frozen corn, peas or mixed vegetables

Yield: 4-6 servings

In a saucepan, combine the rice, water, soup mix and salt; bring to a boil. Add the vegetables; return to a boil. Reduce heat; cover and simmer for 15 minutes. Cook until rice and vegetables are tender.

VANILLA (OR PEACH) ICE CREAM

6	eggs
1	can Eagle Brand milk
1	cup sugar with 2 T. flour mixed in
1	can evaporated milk
1	pint half and half
6-8	peaches, mashed or pureed
3	cups milk, approximately
1	t. vanilla

Yield: 8-10 servings, 2 quarts

Beat eggs well. Add rest of ingredients in order. Fill ice cream freezer with milk up to correct level. Freeze with alternating layers of ice and salt.

Slow-Cooked Pork Ribs
Stuffed Zucchini
Helen's Potato Salad
Easy Peach Cobbler

SLOW-COOKED PORK RIBS

¾-1 cup vinegar
½ cup ketchup
2 T. sugar
2 T. Worcestershire sauce
1 garlic clove, minced
1 t. ground mustard
1 t. paprika
½-1 t. salt
⅛ t. pepper

2 lbs. pork spareribs
1 T. vegetable oil

Yield: 4 servings

Combine the first nine ingredients in a slow cooker. Cut ribs into serving-size pieces; brown in a skillet in oil. Transfer to slow cooker. Cover and cook on low for 4-6 hours or until tender.

STUFFED ZUCCHINI

Wonderful with fresh summer zucchini.

6 small zucchini
1 small onion
¼ c. chopped green pepper
¼ c. breadcrumbs
1 can creamed corn
1 t. leaf thyme
1 t. tarragon
½ t. salt
¼ t. pepper
¼ c. grated Parmesan cheese
1 t. paprika

Yield: 6 servings

Parboil zucchini for 5 minutes. Cut lengthwise in half. Scoop out inside and discard. Sauté onion and pepper in butter. Stir in chopped zucchini. Add rest of ingredients except parmesan cheese. Sprinkle cheese and paprika on top. Bake at 350° for 30 minutes.

HELEN'S POTATO SALAD

6   medium potatos (2 lbs.)
1   lg. jar chopped pimentos
½   cup finely chopped onion
⅓   cup sweet pickles
1¼   cups mayonnaise or salad dressing
2   t. prepared mustard
1½   t. salt
2   hard cooked eggs, coarsely chopped

Yield: 8 servings

In a covered saucepan cook potatoes in boiling salted water for 25 to 30 minutes or until tender; drain well. Peel and cube potatoes. Transfer to a large bowl. Add onion, and sweet pickles. Add mayonnaise or salad dressing, prepared mustard and salt. Toss lightly to coat potato mixture. Carefully fold in the chopped eggs. Cover and chill thoroughly. Before serving sprinkle with paprika.

EASY PEACH COBBLER

½   cup unsalted butter
1   cup all-purpose flour
2   cups sugar, divided
1   T. baking powder
pinch of salt
1   cup milk
4   cups fresh peach slices
1   T. lemon juice
ground cinnamon or nutmeg (optional)

Yield: 10 servings

Melt butter in a 13 x 9 inch baking dish. Combine flour, 1 cup sugar, baking powder, and salt; add milk, stirring just until dry ingredients are moistened. Pour batter over butter (do not stir).

Bring remaining 1 cup sugar, peach slices, and lemon juice to a boil over high heat, stirring constantly; pour over batter (do not stir). Sprinkle with cinnamon or nutmeg if desired.

Bake at 375° for 40 to 45 minutes or until golden brown. Serve cobbler warm or cool.

Parmesan-Artichoke Crostini

Roasted Red Pepper Rollups

Luminarias Salad

Summer Squash with Scallions

Oven Roasted Tomatoes

Pork Tenderloin with Hawaiian Sauce

Mango Margaritas

Chiltons

PARMESAN-ARTICHOKE CROSTINI

1 (14 oz.) can artichoke hearts, drained and chopped
1 (4.5 oz.) can chopped green chilies, drained
2 garlic cloves, minced
1 cup light mayonnaise
1 cup grated Parmesan cheese
40 baguette slices, toasted

Yield: about 3½ dozen

Stir together the first 5 ingredients. Spread 1 tablespoon of mixture on toasted slice of bread and place on ungreased baking sheets.

Bake at 400° for 3 to 5 minutes or until thoroughly heated. Serve immediately.

ROASTED RED PEPPER ROLLUPS

1	7 oz. jar roasted sweet red peppers
4	8 inch flour tortillas
1	3 oz. goat cheese log
1	6 oz. container frozen guacamole, thawed
¼	t. freshly ground pepper
fresh basil (optional for garnish)	

Yield: 2 dozen

Drain the roasted peppers and pat dry with paper towels. Then chop coarsely.

Spread the tortillas evenly with goat cheese and spread guacamole evenly over cheese.

Sprinkle with chopped red pepper and ground pepper. Roll up, pressing edges to seal; cut each roll into 6 slices using a serrated knife. Secure slices with toothpicks. Garnish if desired.

LUMINARIAS SALAD

Salad:
mixed greens of your choice
8-10 radishes (sliced)
1 package of sliced mushrooms
1 medium zucchini (sliced or diced)
1 medium cucumber, diced
½ of head cauliflower, chopped
3-4 medium tomatoes, cut into wedges

Dressing:
1 cup mayonnaise
4 T. prepared mustard
4 T. vinegar
4 T. honey
3 sprigs of parsley, chopped
¼ medium onion, diced fine
pinch of salt
½ t. sugar
½ t. monosodium glutamate (optional)
1 cup vegetable oil

Yield: 8-salads

Combine all ingredients except oil. Mix together then add oil stirring constantly.

SUMMER SQUASH WITH SCALLIONS

12-16 scallions or green onions
2   t. sesame oil
2   t. olive oil
2   t. soy sauce
¼   t. ground ginger
¼   t. sugar
¼   t. red pepper flakes
¾   pound yellow squash, zucchini or a mixture of the two
4   oz. fresh mushrooms, sliced

Yields: 4 servings

Trim roots from scallions and pull off tough outer layer. Cut off all but 2 inches of their green tops. Place in a 1 quart casserole along with the oils, soy sauce, ginger, sugar and pepper. Toss to coat. Cover with lid or vented plastic wrap and microwave on high for 2 minutes.

Cut squash crosswise into 2 inch chunks, then cut chunks into 4 to 6 sticks each. Add squash and mushrooms to onions; cover. Stirring midway through cooking, microwave on high 4 minutes or until squash is crispy tender.

OVEN ROASTED TOMATOES

6   Roma tomatoes, sliced ½ inch thick
3   T. olive oil
3-4   cloves garlic, sliced thinly
1   t. fresh ground black pepper
2   t. balsamic vinegar

Yield: 24 slices

Preheat oven to 350°. Place tomatoes in a mixing bowl, with remaining ingredients and toss to distribute ingredients.

Spread on a baking sheet in a single layer. Place in oven for 15 to 20 minutes until the tomatoes are bubbly and just tender.

Remove from oven and let cool. Store in container in the refrigerator. Be sure to keep the juices too.

PORK TENDERLOIN WITH HAWAIIAN SAUCE

Fabulous!

2 pound tenderloin

Pork Tenderloin Rub:
3   T. brown sugar
2   t. garlic powder
2   t. chili powder
½-1 t. black pepper
½   t. oregano leaves
½   t. salt

Yield: 6 servings

Sprinkle tenderloin generously with garlic salt and fresh ground pepper.

Combine all other ingredients and coat tenderloin. Refrigerate for 3 hours. Grill for 30 to 35 minutes. The last 5 minutes of cooking, baste the loin with the prepared sauce. Use the additional sauce to top each portion of pork.

Hawaiian Sauce:
2   cups pork stock (see below)
½   cup yellow mustard
½   cup Creole mustard
2-3 T. honey
½   cup horseradish
½   cup catsup
½   cup dark brown sugar
1½   t. minced garlic
¼   cup white wine

Combine all the ingredients in a saucepan. Simmer 20 minutes.

Pork Loin Stock:
pork loin bone
1   large onion, roughly
     chopped
1   carrot, diced
1   rib celery, diced
black peppercorns
pinch of salt
water

Chop the bone into several pieces, then place it in a large pot with the onion, carrot, celery, black peppercorns and pinch of salt. Add water to cover. Bring the liquid to a boil, reduce the heat, and simmer until it has reduced by half. Strain through a fine sieve into a smaller sauce pan. Continue to simmer until the liquid has reduced to about 3 cups. Cool, then refrigerate until ready to use. Remove and discard the fat layer that forms on the top. Use in the Hawaiian Sauce.

MANGO MARGARITAS

1 (26 oz.) jar sliced
mangoes
1 (5 oz.) frozen limeade
1 cup gold tequila
½ cup Triple Sec or
Cointreau
¼ cup Grand Marnier
colored sugar (optional for rim
of glasses)

Yield: 10 cups

Spoon 3 tablespoons mango liquid into saucer, pour mangoes and remaining liquid into blender. Add limeade and next 3 ingredients and blend. Pour half into a pitcher, set aside. Add ice to remaining liquid and blend. Repeat with remaining mango mixture.

Place sugar in a saucer. Dip rims of glasses into mango juice and then into sugar for a pretty glass.

CHILTONS

The Fabulous Five drink of choice.
We enjoy this drink year round
but it is a super summer cocktail.

Lemons
Salt for glass rim
Vodka
Soda
Ice

Salt the rim of a tall cocktail glass.

Squeeze the juice of ½ lemon (small) into the glass.

Fill the glass with ice.

Add a shot and ½ of vodka (your favorite).

Fill up glass with soda.

Add a ¼ wedge of lemon juice and drop lemon into glass.

Enjoy!!!!

FAB FIVE FOOTNOTES

Salad success: Be sure lettuce is cold, crisp and dry. Tear, don't cut lettuce into bite-size pieces. Add dressing just before serving.

Before using the grill for the first time of the season, make sure the grill top itself is clean and, if it's a gas grill, all fittings are tight.

Before putting any food onto the fire, an even bed of coals should be covered in gray ash; this takes about 45 minutes from the time the fire is lit. Food to be grilled should be at room temperature to help even cooking.

Use long-handled tools to prevent burns (the tools needed are a fork, turner, tongs that spring back on their own, and a basting brush) and use oven mitts.

Always keep a spray bottle handy to spritz out flare-ups.

Brushing the food to be cooked lightly with oil will help to prevent sticking.

NOTES

UNDER THE SEA

"Laughter is brightest where food is best."
Irish Proverb

UNDER THE SEA

Twice a year, we take a trip together to get away from our busy routines. We talk, laugh, cry, eat, shop, and, of course, we cook. Each year our friendship deepens, and we know more about each other and ourselves. In all of our travels, from Fredericksburg, Texas, to other interesting places like Las Vegas, Nevada; Santa Fe, New Mexico; and Branson, Missouri, we always find a way to put cooking into our trip. One elaborate, homemade lunch—complete with matching paper plates and napkins and Bloody Marys—was graciously served by Southwest Airline flight attendants on our way to Carmel, California.

Of all our outings, the unanimous favorite is our 1997 journey to Carmel. We stayed in a beautiful home with an ocean-front view and made it our mission to try every seafood dish available. For landlocked West Texans, seafood is always an exotic adventure, and we are always ready to discover a new variety and a new way to prepare and serve this wonderful gift from the sea.

This chapter is a collection of our seafood menus and recipes. We have developed them from the fresh fish selection availabe in West Texas, which until very lately, has been rather limited. Nevertheless, these meals are delicious and are sure to please seafood aficionados and novices alike.

Baked Tomatoes
Shrimp & Wild Rice Casserole
Blueberry-Cream Cheese Squares

BAKED TOMATOES

8   tomatoes
½   cup sour cream
½   cup mayonnaise
1   t. curry powder
1   T. fresh parsley
salt & pepper to taste

Yield: 8 servings

Slice off top of tomatoes and remove about half of the pulp. Mix the next five (5) ingredients and add the tomato pulp. Stuff the tomatoes with the mixture. Top with dry bread crumbs. Bake at 350° for 20 – 30 minutes.

"Life itself is the proper binge"
Julia Child

SHRIMP & WILD RICE CASSEROLE

*Fabulous casserole! Expensive to make
but absolutely worth every dime.*

2   lbs. shrimp, cooked &
      deveined
½   stick butter
4   green onions, tops &
      bottoms, chopped
1   clove garlic
1   small green pepper,
      chopped
2   pkgs. Uncle Ben's Long
      Grain & Wild Rice, cooked
      as package directs
2   cans Cream of Chicken
      Soup
1   cup mayonnaise
Small jar chopped pimentos
1   16 oz. can green beans,
      well drained
1   5-oz. can water chestnuts,
      sliced & drained
1   cup Monterey Jack cheese,
      grated
1   cup Cheddar cheese,
      grated
½   cup Parmesan cheese,
      grated
1   cup buttered bread crumbs
Dash each Tabasco &
      Worcestershire
Salt & Pepper to taste

Yield: 12 servings

In saucepan, sauté the onions, garlic and green pepper until soft. Combine remaining ingredients, except bread crumbs; mix until well blended. Pour into greased 13 × 9 Pyrex dish. Top with buttered bread crumbs and bake at 350° for 30 minutes. Will Freeze.

BLUEBERRY-CREAM CHEESE SQUARES

1½ cups graham cracker crumbs
½ cup powdered sugar
1 stick butter, melted
1 cup sugar
1 21-oz. can blueberry pie filling
1 8-oz. pkg. cream cheese, room temperature
2 eggs, beaten to blend
2½ T. fresh lemon juice

Yield: 12-15 servings

Preheat oven to 350°. Butter a 9 x 13 inch baking dish. Mix crumbs, powdered sugar and butter in medium bowl. Press into bottom of prepared dish using fork. Mix sugar, cream cheese and eggs in medium bowl until smooth. Spread over crust. Bake 20 minutes. Cool. Stir lemon juice into pie filling. Spread over cheese mixture. Cover tightly and refrigerate. Cut into squares to serve.

159

Cajun Shrimp Boil
Crusty French Bread
Cheese Cake Brownies

CAJUN SHRIMP BOIL

Great fun for outdoor dining.
A one pot feast!

3 quarts water
2 lbs. unpeeled large shrimp
3 large onions, quartered
6 new potatoes, unpeeled
1 lb. polski kielbasa sausage, cut into 1 inch pieces
6 ears shucked corn, each cut crosswise into 4 pieces
1 box crawfish, shrimp, and crab boil (such as Zatarain's)

Yield: 8 servings

Boil potatoes until soft. Bring water and seasoning bag to a boil in an 8-quart stock pot; cook 10 minutes. Add sausage and onion; cook 5 minutes. Add corn and potatoes; cook 5 minutes. Add shrimp; cook 3 minutes or until shrimp are done. Open seasoning bag to disperse spices into water. Spices will adhere to shrimp and veggies and add more color to the dish.

Drain and put in large serving bowl. For easy cleanup, use paper bags or newspaper for plates and eat without utensils!

CRUSTY FRENCH BREAD

CHEESE CAKE BROWNIES

4	T. unsalted butter (plus more for pan)
¾	cup flour
¾	t. baking powder
¼	t. salt
6	oz. bittersweet chocolate, chopped
5	large whole eggs plus 2 large egg yolks
1⅓	cups sugar
1½	t. pure vanilla extract
1	pound mascarpone cheese

(Cream cheese may be substituted for mascarpone but the topping will be dense and tangy instead of mellow and creamy. If using cream cheese, reduce baking time by ten minutes.)

Yields: about 5 dozen

Heat oven to 350°. Butter a 9 x 13 inch baking pan and line with parchment. Whisk together flour, baking powder and salt, and set aside. In the top of a barely simmering double boiler, melt together chocolate and butter. Remove from heat.

In the bowl of an electric mixer fitted with the whisk attachment, beat together 3 eggs and 1 cup sugar on high speed until thick and fluffy, about 5 minutes. On low speed, add reserved chocolate mixture and 1 t. vanilla extract. When combined, add flour mixture. Stir until just combined. Spread mixture evenly into prepared pan. Set aside.

In the clean bowl of the electric mixer fitted with the paddle attachment, beat together mascarpone cheese, remaining eggs and yolks, remaining sugar and remaining vanilla on medium speed, until smooth. Pour over chocolate mixture. Bake until cheese mixture is golden and set, about 35 minutes. Transfer to a wire rack to cool completely. Cut into about 60 – 1-by-1½ inch pieces.

Creamy Shrimp Dip

Herbed Asparagus with Parmesan Cheese

Steamed Potatoes

Poached Salmon with Lemon Dill Sauce

Banana Caramel Pie

CREAMY SHRIMP DIP

Great for a crowd

1   cup mayonnaise
1   t. onion flakes, crushed
1   t. chopped parsley
½   t. dried dill
½   t. celery salt
1   cup sour cream
8   oz. canned shrimp, chopped

Yield: 12 appetizer servings

Mix all ingredients. Chill for 2 hours. Serve with corn chips or crackers.

HERBED ASPARAGUS WITH PARMESAN CHEESE

2 lbs. Pencil-thin asparagus, trimmed
4 T. unsalted butter, at room temperature
1 T. chopped fresh parsley
1 T. snipped fresh chives
1 T. chopped fresh dill
1 T. chopped fresh rosemary
1 t. coarsely ground black pepper
4 oz. Parmesan cheese

Yield: 6 servings

Bring a large pot of water to a boil, and add the asparagus.

Simmer until just tender, 1½ to 2 minutes. Drain and pat dry.

Combine the butter, chopped herbs and pepper in a small bowl and blend thoroughly.

Just before serving, melt the herb butter over medium heat in a large heavy skillet. Add the asparagus and toss gently to heat through, 2 minutes.

Transfer the asparagus to a warmed serving platter and shave Parmesan cheese over it. Serve immediately.

STEAMED POTATOES

12 very small red new potatoes
1 cup water
1 T. unsalted butter
Coarse Kosher salt, to taste
Coarsely ground black pepper, to taste
1 T. fresh Italian (flat-leaf) parsley or fresh dill
1 t. paprika

Yield: 4 servings

If you like, use a vegetable peeler to remove a thin stripe of red skin around the center of each potato; even it off with a small paring knife if necessary.

Place the potatoes and water in a saucepan and bring to a boil. Reduce the heat to medium, cover and cook, shaking the pan occasionally, until the potatoes are tender, 30 minutes.

Drain the potatoes and return them to the saucepan. Shake it over low heat to remove the remaining moisture, 10-15 seconds. Then remove the pan from the heat, add the butter, salt, pepper and parsley, paprika and toss well. Transfer the potatoes to bowl and serve immediately.

POACHED SALMON

Prepare a wine court bouillon:

1	onion, sliced
1	carrot, sliced
1	celery rib, sliced
1	T. dried parsley
1	T. dried thyme
1	T. dill
1	bay leaf
2	cup dry white wine
10	pepercorn

Add the vegetables, parsley, thyme, dill and a bay leaf to about 1-quart of salted water. Simmer, uncovered for 15 minutes, then add dry white wine. Cover and simmer for 15 minutes more, adding peppercorns for the last 10 minutes. Strain before using.

To prepare salmon:

Lower salmon fillets into the court bouillon. The bouillon should never boil. Usually allow 10 minutes cooking time for each inch of thickness. Salmon should be opaque throughout when done. Serve with mustard dill sauce.

Mustard Dill Sauce:

1½	T. white wine vinegar
1¾	T. sugar
½	cup olive oil
5-6	T. Dijon mustard
1	T. chopped fresh dill
1	heaping T. freshly ground white pepper

Whisk the vinegar and sugar together in a small mixing bowl until the sugar has dissolved. Slowly add the olive oil, whisking well until all the oil is incorporated. Blend in the mustard and chopped dill and season with the white pepper. Cover and refrigerate until needed.

BANANA CARAMEL PIE

This is so good and so easy!

2 cans Sweetened
   Condensed Milk
   (caramelized)
1 pie shell, prebaked
2 medium to large bananas
Cool Whip
Pecans or chopped Heath
   candy bar

Yield: 8 servings

To make caramelized Condensed milk ahead, boil several cans with label removed for 3 hours. During the 3 hours of cooking, always keep the cans covered with water. Store extra cans in pantry for quick dessert.

Add sliced bananas to baked pie shell. Top with Caramelized condensed milk. Add Cool Whip and sprinkle with topping. Refrigerate.

Hot Clam Dip
Shrimp Etouffe
Creamed Spinach
Ice Cream Pie to Die For

HOT CLAM DIP

2	8 oz. pkgs. cream cheese, softened
1	6½ oz. can minced clams, undrained
1	t. Creole seasoning
½	clove garlic, crushed

Juice of 1 lemon
Paprika

Yield: 8 appetizer servings

Combine all ingredients except paprika in a medium saucepan; cook over low heat, stirring constantly, until mixture is smooth and well heated. Sprinkle with paprika. Serve warm with crackers.

SHRIMP ETOUFFE

1½	cup onion, chopped
⅔	cup green pepper, chopped
⅔	cup celery, chopped
4	T. butter
2	large cloves garlic, minced
1	T. lemon juice
½	T. Worcestershire sauce
1	T. cornstarch
½	T. Creole seasoning
1	lb. Shrimp, cleaned and deveined

Rice or noodles

Yield: 4 servings

Place onion, pepper, celery, butter and garlic in a 2-quart round casserole; cover. Microwave on high 10 minutes or until vegetables are transparent, stirring midway through cooking.

Combine lemon juice, Worcestershire sauce, cornstarch and Creole seasoning. Stir into vegetable mixture along with the shrimp; cover. Microwave on high 5½ to 6 minutes or until shrimp are opaque, stirring midway through cooking. Serve over rice or noodles.

CREAMED SPINACH

1 lb. fresh spinach
1½ T. butter
1½ T. flour
¾ cup milk
Salt & pepper to taste

Yield: 4 servings

Wash and dry spinach, chop. Place spinach in a 2-quart casserole, cover. Microwave on high 4-5 minutes. Let stand covered while preparing sauce.

Put butter into 4-cup glass measure. Microwave on high 30 seconds or until melted. Use a wire whisk to blend in flour, then add milk to the butter. Whisking midway though cooking, microwave on high 2-3 minutes, or until thickened. Stir in salt & pepper. Mix with spinach.

ICE CREAM PIE TO DIE FOR

1¼ cup Graham cracker crumbs
3 T. sugar
⅓ cup butter, melted
1 quart butter pecan ice cream, softened
1 16 oz. can chocolate fudge topping
1½ cup chopped pecan, toasted
1 quart pralines & cream ice cream, softened

Yield: 8 servings

Combine graham cracker crumbs, sugar and butter, mix well. Firmly press mixture into bottom of a 9-inch springform pan. Bake at 350° for 8 minutes. Cool completely.

Spread butter pecan ice cream evenly over crust; cover and freeze. Spread half of fudge topping over ice cream; sprinkle with ½ cup pecans. Cover pie and freeze.

Spread pralines and cream ice cream evenly over pie; cover and freeze until ice cream is firm. Just before serving, spoon remaining fudge topping into a heavy saucepan; heat just until thoroughly heated. To serve, drizzle warm fudge topping over each slice of pie and sprinkle with remaining pecans.

To toast pecans, heat at 350° for 10 minutes.

Spicy Oriental Soup

Hot and Sour Shrimp with Watercress and Walnuts

Cheese Sticks

Rice Pudding

SPICY ORIENTAL SOUP

4	dried black mushrooms (available in Oriental markets)
5	cups chicken broth
1	chicken breast half, skinned, boned and diced
¼	cup bamboo shoots, slivered
½	cup rice vinegar
2	T. soy sauce
1	scallion, including top, cut into 2-inch slivers
1	t. finely chopped cilantro
1	t. hot pepper sauce
½	t. salt
½	t. white pepper
3	T. cornstarch mixed with ¼ cup water
1	egg, slightly beaten

Yield: 4-6 servings

Soak mushrooms in warm water covered for 30 minutes, drain. Cut off and discard stems and thinly slice caps. Set aside.

Bring broth to boil over medium-high heat in large saucepan. Add chicken and cook, stirring occasionally for 3 minutes. Stir in mushrooms, bamboo shoots, vinegar, soy sauce, green onion, cilantro, hot pepper sauce, salt and white pepper. Return to boil. Add cornstarch mixture and cook, stirring, until soup slightly thickens. Remove pot from heat and slowly drizzle in eggs, stirring constantly. Serve immediately.

HOT AND SOUR SHRIMP WITH WATERCRESS AND WALNUTS

This is spicy & delicious!

1 lb. large uncooked shrimp; peeled, deveined and butterflied
4 T. dry Sherry
1 T. fresh ginger, peeled and grated
½ cup chicken stock or canned broth
2 T. soy sauce
2 T. catsup
1 T. cornstarch
1 T. rice vinegar or white wine vinegar
1 T. sugar
1 t. oriental sesame oil
¼ t. cayenne pepper
6 t. peanut oil
2 T. chopped walnuts
3 bunches watercress, trimmed
2 medium red bell peppers, cut into 1-inch squares
2 garlic cloves, minced
8 green onions, cut diagonally into 1-inch-long pieces

Yield: 4-6 servings

Combine shrimp, 2 T. sherry and ginger in large bowl. Cover and refrigerate for 30 minutes. Mix remaining 2 T. sherry, chicken stock, soy sauce, catsup, cornstarch, rice vinegar, sugar, sesame oil and cayenne pepper in small bowl.

Heat 2 t. peanut oil in wok or heavy large skillet over high heat. Add walnuts and stir-fry one minute. Transfer walnuts to plate using slotted spoon. Add watercress to wok and stir-fry until just wilted, about 1 minute. Divide watercress among plates. Add 2 t. peanut oil, bell peppers and garlic to wok and stir-fry 1 minute. Add remaining 2 t. peanut oil, shrimp mixture and onions and stir-fry 1 minute. Stir stock mixture, add to wok and cook sauce until clear and thick, stirring frequently, 2 minutes.

Spoon sauce and shrimp over watercress. Sprinkle with walnuts and serve.

CHEESE STICKS

1   loaf regular sliced bread, crust removed
½   cup margarine, melted
1   cup Parmesan cheese
1   t. paprika

Yield: 10 servings

Slice bread into thin 1" strips. Roll in melted margarine, then in Parmesan and paprika. Place on cookie sheet. Bake at 325° for 20 minutes.

RICE PUDDING

2   cups skim milk, heated
2   cups cooked white rice
⅓   cup sugar
1½   t. vanilla
¼   t. nutmeg
½   t. cinnamon
1   egg, beaten
1½   t. grated lemon rind, optional
½   t. lemon extract, optional

Yield: 8 servings

Preheat oven to 350°. Whisk all ingredients together. Pour into greased casserole dish with lid. Place casserole dish in a pan with one-inch deep hot water. Bake one hour.

"Food is the first enjoyment of life."

Lin Yutang

Salmon Mousse
Blackened Carpaccio with Chili Mayonnaise
Grilled Prawns with Papaya Salsa
Miriam's Pineapple Cake

SALMON MOUSSE

1 envelope unflavored gelatin
¼ cup cold water
½ cup boiling water
½ cup Hellmann's mayonnaise
1 T. lemon juice
1 T. finely grated onion
Dash of Tabasco
¼ t. sweet paprika
1 t. salt
2 T. finely chopped dill
2 cups finely flaked poached fresh or canned salmon, skin and bones removed
1 cup heavy cream

Yield: 12 servings

Soften the gelatin in the cold water in large mixing bowl. Stir in the boiling water and whisk the mixture slowly until gelatin dissolves. Cool to room temperature.

Whisk in the mayonnaise, lemon juice, grated onion, Tabasco, paprika, salt and dill. Stir to blend completely and refrigerate for about 20 minutes or until the mixture begins to thicken slightly.

Fold in the finely flaked salmon. In a separate bowl, whip the cream until it is thickened to peaks and fluffy. Fold gently into the salmon mixture.

Transfer the mixture to a 6 to 8 cup bowl or decorative mold. Cover and chill for at least 4 hours.

Serve on toasts, black bread or crackers. Or serve as a first course, garnished with watercress.

BLACKENED CARPACCIO WITH CHILI MAYONNAISE

2 T. paprika
2 T. freshly ground white pepper
1 T. dried basil
1 T. cayenne pepper
1 T. chili powder
1 T. ground cumin
1 T. garlic powder
1 T. onion powder
1 T. dried leaf oregano
1 T. salt
1¼ pounds beef tenderloin, well trimmed
3 T. clarified butter
Lettuce leaves
Chili mayonnaise (recipe follows)
2 firm tomatoes, chopped
6 sprigs fresh cilantro for garnish

Mix spices together in bottom of large flat dish. Dip beef in butter, then roll in spices mixture until beef is heavily coated on all sides.

Heat large heavy skillet, preferably, cast-iron, over medium high heat until very hot. Put beef into skillet (turn fan on as this will smoke.) Cook until one side is blackened, about 5 minutes. Immediately turn and cook until blackened all around. Remove to plate; refrigerate immediately. (Beef will be blackened outside and very rare inside.) Refrigerate until thoroughly cold, 2 to 3 hours.

Arrange lettuce leaves in single layer over 6 chilled dinner plates. Using an electric knife, cut beef into very thin slices. Arrange slices over lettuce.

Top each serving with dollop of chili mayonnaise. Garnish with tomato and cilantro.

CHILI MAYONNAISE

1 cup mayonnaise
½ t. cayenne pepper
¼ t. chili powder
1 jalapeño pepper, seeded and minced

Yield: 12 appetizer servings

Mix mayonnaise, cayenne pepper, chili powder and jalapeño together in small bowl. Cover and refrigerate until needed.

GRILLED PRAWNS WITH PAPAYA SALSA

18   jumbo prawns, peeled except for the tail and deveined
¼   cup vegetable oil
Juice of 1 medium lime
½   cup chopped fresh cilantro
4   green onions with some of the green, coarsely chopped
3   small avocados, peeled, pitted and thinly sliced
Papaya salsa

Place prawns in a glass bowl. In another bowl, whisk together oil, lime juice, cilantro and green onions, and pour the mixture over prawns. Cover and marinate for 1 hour at room temperature.

Prepare grill until coals are ash-covered. Grill prawns on skewers (3 per skewer) 4 inches from coals until opaque, about 2 minutes per side. To serve fan out avocado slices on individual plates, prawns, and garnish with papaya salsa.

PAPAYA SALSA

1   medium papaya, peeled, seeded and finely diced
1   medium red bell pepper, finely diced
6   green onions, finely diced
½   cup chopped fresh cilantro
1-2   small jalapeños, seeded and minced
Juice of 2 medium limes
½   t. salt

Yield: 6 servings

Combine ingredients in a bowl and toss to mix.

MIRIAM'S PINEAPPLE CAKE

Yellow box cake mix
(follow directions for 2
layer cake)

Filling:
1½ cup sugar
2 T. cornstarch
½ t. salt

Stir in:
¾ cup pineapple juice
1 cup crushed pineapple
Bring to a boil and cook until
thick and clear, several
minutes.

Add:
1 T. butter
1 t. lemon juice
Cool

Seven minutes frosting (recipe
follows)

Put filling between layers and
save ½ cup of filling for the center
of top.

Frost cake, sides and top.

In center of top spoon remaining
filling, leave 1-2 inches around
sides of cake.

SEVEN MINUTE FROSTING

1½ cups sugar
½ cup water
2 egg whites
1 T. light corn syrup
Dash of salt
1 t. vanilla

Yield: about 5⅓ cups

Mix sugar, water, egg whites,
corn syrup and salt in top of
double boiler.

Beat about 1 minute to blend
thoroughly. Place over boiling

water. Beat constantly with
electric mixer on high speed until
frosting stands in stiff peaks;
about 7 minutes, scraping sides
occasionally with rubber scraper.

Remove from boiling water.
Immediately pour into large
bowl. Add vanilla; beat until
thick enough to spread, about 1
minute.

FAB FIVE FOOTNOTES

Thyme added to butter for baking and broiling all seafoods and chicken is delicious.

If you doubt the freshness of a fish, place it in cold water; if it floats it has recently been caught.

Always cook fish slow and at a low to moderate temperature. Never more than 350°.

Lemon juice rubbed on fish before cooking will enhance the flavor and help maintain a good color.

When frying fish, sprinkle the bottom of the pan with a small amount of salt and the fish won't stick to the pan.

To remove fish odor from hands, rub hands with salt and wash with cold water.

NOTES

HOLIDAY EXTRAVAGANZAS

Excellent wine generates enthusiasm.
And whatever you do with enthusiasm
is generally successful.

HOLIDAY EXTRAVAGANZAS

This chapter of our cookbook contains all of the menus and recipes from our Christmas Progressive Dinners. Our first Christmas Progressive Dinner was in 1987 when we transformed our new monthly routine into a gala event that included our husbands. It was at that first progressive dinner that we initiated the special apron of the Fabulous Five.

At our November dinner of that first year, Jan asked us to bring our high school annuals to share our memories, and Debbie had a memory that put us in stitches, literally, as it turned out. In the 1970s, she was a bridesmaid in a wedding that boasted dresses bedecked with different colors of ostrich feathers. At our first Christmas Progressive Dinner that next month, we were thrilled to find that Phyllis had made an apron trimmed with red ostrich feathers for the hostess to wear. We carried it with us from house to house for each of us to add to our apparel as hostess. In 2000, we celebrated our 14th annual progressive dinner, and the apron was still a part of the festivities. It is a tradition at every Christmas dinner. In 1999, Jan put new ostrich feathers on our special apron, and we're confident it's good for another fourteen years.

Now that our group is spread between Lubbock and Fort Worth, what began as a special evening of dining in Lubbock has evolved into a holiday season family weekend, rotating between hometowns. The gathering is full of cooking, eating, shopping, gift giving, special activities for the children, and other family surprises. We have had appetizers in the Van Cliburn suite at the Fort Worth Worthington Hotel—complete with pianist—and trolley rides in Lubbock for all seventeen of us to look at Christmas lights.

Our traditional Christmas Progressive Dinner with our husbands continues to be a gastronomic event of epic proportions and the highlights of our holiday reunions. We have hired a limousine to take us from house to house, and even commissioned Christmas carolers and musicians to entertain us while we dine. The meal takes hours. We savor every course as we celebrate our rich lives together.

The menus from these dinners are designed to create splendid affairs, so plan ahead and polish up all of your best dinnerware to add the final flourish. The elegance of the meal will do you proud.

Smoked Salmon Torte

Raspberry Cheese Spread

Turkey

Cranberry Apple Salad

Butternut Squash Soup

*Souffled Sweet Potatoes
with Brandy Cream Sauce*

*Green Beans with Roquefort Cheese
and Walnuts*

Cornbread Dressing

Chocolate Pecan Pie

*Pumpkin Cheesecake Pie
with Cornmeal Crust*

A true holiday feast!

SMOKED SALMON TORTE

Torte Layers:
4   T. butter
½   cup flour
2   cups milk
4   egg yolks
1   t. sugar
⅛   t. salt
4   egg whites
⅛   t. cream of tartar

Smoked Salmon Layer:
8   oz. cream cheese
½   cup sour cream
2   T. fresh lemon juice
¼   cup chopped green onions
⅓   pound smoked salmon, shredded (reserve 1 T. for garnish)
¼   cup peeled and chopped cucumber
¼   t. dried dill weed or
1   T. fresh dill weed

Sour Cream Frosting:
½   pint sour cream
1   t. onion powder
1   T. fresh lemon juice

Garnish:
1   T. smoked salmon
pitted black olives (sliced)
chives or green onion tops
sprigs of fresh dill or parsley

Yields: 12 servings

To prepare torte layers, melt butter in small saucepan. Stir in flour and cook over low heat until well blended, about 2 minutes: do not brown. Stir in milk and continue cooking until sauce comes to a boil and thickens. In small bowl, lightly whisk egg yolks, sugar and salt. Stir small amount of hot mixture into yolks; stir yolks into saucepan. Cook for 1 minute, stirring constantly. Remove from heat. Beat egg whites until frothy, add cream of tartar, and beat until stiff peaks form. Fold sauce into whites.

Line bottoms of 2-9 inch layer cake pans with rounds of waxed paper; grease paper and sides of pans. Divide torte mixture between 2 pans; spreading evenly. Bake at 350° for 15 minutes; rotate cakes and bake for an additional 20 to 25 minutes or until lightly browned and top springs back when pressed. Cool in pans for 10 minutes. Invert onto cake racks and pull off paper. Cool completely.

To prepare salmon filling, beat cream cheese, sour cream and lemon juice with electric mixer until smooth. Add green onions, salmon, cucumber and dill weed. Mix until blended.

Place one torte on serving platter and spread with filling. Place second torte on filling. Several hours before serving, mix all frosting ingredients together until smooth. Frost torte and decorate top with smoked salmon, olives, chives and green onions. Garnish with sprigs of fresh dill or parsley. Cut like a cake to serve.

RASPBERRY CHEESE SPREAD

2½ cups shredded New York white cheddar cheese
⅓ cup grated onion
2 T. mayonnaise
½ cup raspberry preserves
Triscuit wafers

Yields: 2 cups

In mixing bowl, combine cheese and onion and mix well. Blend in mayonnaise. Form into a flat mound on serving dish and top with preserves. Serve with Triscuit wafers.

TURKEY

Roasting a Turkey

Place your turkey in a roasting pan, breast side up. Use a roasting pan large enough to baste easily.

To ensure that the skin browns crisply, smear the bird all over with vegetable oil or butter.

Baste the turkey with the natural juices every 15-20 minutes to help brown the skin.

Cook the turkey according to the chart below at 325°.

To test for doneness, push a skewer deeply into the thickest part of a thigh. If the juices that run out are clear, the bird is done; if not, roast 10 more minutes.

If you find that the breast is brown before the bird is cooked through, shield the breast by covering it with a loose sheet of aluminum foil.

Let the turkey set up 20-30 minutes before carving.

Pounds	Roasting Time
5-12	2-3 hours
12-18	3-4 hours
18-25	4-5 hours

CRANBERRY APPLE SALAD

1½ cups cranberries,
    coarsely chopped
3   T. sugar
2   T. fresh lime juice
2   t. Dijon mustard
½   cup virgin olive oil
1   cup walnuts, chopped
2   large Granny Smith
    apples, cored and coarsely
    chopped
¼   cup sliced green onions
1   head romaine lettuce
freshly grated lime peel
    (garnish)

Yields: 6-8 serving

In a small bowl, combine cranberries and sugar. Cover and refrigerate overnight.

In a medium bowl, mix lime juice and mustard. Add oil in slow stream, beating constantly. Marinate walnuts, apples and onions in the dressing for 1 to 4 hours.

To serve, line a large bowl with romaine leaves. Spoon apple mixture over leaves. Make a well in the middle of apple mixture and spoon in cranberry mixture. Garnish with grated lime peel.

BUTTERNUT SQUASH SOUP

2   cups chopped onion
2   T. butter
2   T. flour
3   cups chicken stock
4   cups fresh butternut
    squash
salt (to taste)
white pepper (to taste)
2   t. nutmeg
1   cup heavy cream
1   cup crabmeat
toasted pumpkin seeds
    (garnish)

Yields: 8-10 servings

Cut squash in half and scoop out the flesh. Cook the squash in the chicken stock until tender. Sauté the onions in the butter until soft. Add flour and continue stirring over low heat (2 minutes). Add chicken stock, squash, and seasonings. Cook on low heat for 10 minutes.

Puree this mixture until smooth. Return the soup to the saucepan and add the cream.

Cook until hot and stir in the crabmeat just before serving. Garnish the soup with the pumpkin seeds.

SOUFFLED SWEET POTATOES WITH BRANDY CREAM SAUCE

2	cups sweet potatoes (4 to 5 potatoes)
1	cup sugar
½	cup butter
8	egg yolks, beaten
1	orange (peel and juice)
1	lemon (peel and juice)
¼	t. ground mace
¼	t. ground cinnamon
¼	t. ground allspice
¼	t. ground nutmeg
½	cup dry sherry
8	egg whites, stiffly beaten

Yields: 10 servings

Peel and quarter sweet potatoes. Cook in boiling water to cover until tender. Drain well and mash. In large mixing bowl, cream together sugar, butter and egg yolks. Stir in mashed potatoes, orange and lemon peels and juices, mace, cinnamon, allspice, nutmeg and sherry. Fold beaten egg whites into potato mixture. Pour into buttered 2 quart soufflé dish. Bake at 350° for 50 minutes or until set.

Serve with Brandy Cream Sauce

BRANDY CREAM SAUCE

2	T. butter
2	T. flour
¾	cup milk
salt and pepper (to taste)	
2	T. brandy
1	orange (juice of)
1½	t. powdered sugar
ground nutmeg	

Yield: 1 cup

In medium saucepan, melt butter and stir in flour. Add milk, whisking constantly. Season to taste with salt. Stir in brandy, orange juice and powdered sugar. Simmer for 2 to 3 minutes or until sauce thickens slightly. Pour into serving bowl and sprinkle with nutmeg.

GREEN BEANS WITH ROQUEFORT CHEESE AND WALNUTS

1 pound fresh green beans
4 strips thick-sliced bacon
4 oz. Roquefort cheese, crumbled
1½ cups walnut halves (toasted)
freshly ground black pepper (to taste)

Yields: 4 servings

Bring a saucepan of water to a boil, and add the beans. Simmer until crisp-tender, about 10 minutes. Drain, rinse under cold water and drain again. Set them aside.

Cut the bacon slices into ¼ inch wide strips. Place them in a skillet and cook over medium heat until well cooked, 5 to 7 minutes. Remove the bacon with a slotted spoon (reserve the grease) and set it aside to drain on paper towels.

Add the green beans to the skillet and heat through over medium heat, for 2 minutes. Add the Roquefort and toss until the cheese just begins to melt, about 30 seconds. Sprinkle with the walnuts and lots of pepper and serve immediately.

CORNBREAD DRESSING

1 recipe of your favorite cornbread
1 package of Pepperidge Farm breadcrumbs
1½-2 cups chopped celery
1-1½ cups chopped onions
1 stick of butter
½ bunch fresh sage (chopped) or dried sage (to taste)
3-4 cans of chicken broth
salt and pepper (to taste)

Sauté the celery and onion in the butter. In a large casserole dish crumble the cornbread. Add the breadcrumbs, the sautéed mixture, sage, and salt and pepper. Mix the above with the chicken broth. Start with 2 to 3 cans and add the last can as needed to make the mixture moist. Bake at 375° for 30 to 40 minutes.

CHOCOLATE PECAN PIE

1 package (8 squares) Baker's semi-Sweet Baking chocolate
1 refrigerated pie crust
2 T. butter
3 eggs, slightly beaten
¼ cup firmly packed light brown sugar
1 cup Karo light or dark corn syrup
1 t. vanilla
1½ cups pecan halves or walnut pieces

Yields: 8 servings

Heat oven to 350°. Coarsely chop 4 squares of the chocolate and set aside. Line 9 inch pie plate with the pie crust. Microwave remaining 4 squares of chocolate and butter in large microwavable bowl on high 1 to 2 minutes or until butter is melted. Stir until chocolate is completely melted. Brush bottom of pie crust with small amount of beaten egg. Stir sugar, corn syrup, eggs and vanilla into chocolate mixture until well blended. Stir in pecans or walnuts and chopped chocolate. Pour into pie crust. Bake 55 minutes or until knife inserted 2 inches from the edge comes out clean. Cool on wire rack.

"There is no such thing as a little garlic."

Arthur Baer

PUMPKIN CHEESECAKE PIE WITH CORNMEAL CRUST

Crust:

3	T. (or more) ice water
1	large egg yolk
1⅓	cups flour
¼	cup yellow cornmeal
1	T. sugar
½	t. salt
½	cup chilled unsalted butter (cut into ½ inch pieces)

Filling:

6	oz. cream cheese, room temperature
½	cup sugar
½	cup packed brown sugar
2	large eggs
1	large egg yolk
1	cup canned pure pumpkin
¾	cup half and half
1	t. ground cinnamon
1	t. ground nutmeg
½	t. grated lemon peel
½	t. ground ginger
¼	t. salt

Yield: 8 servings

For crust:

Whisk 3 T. ice water and egg yolk in small bowl to blend. Mix flour, yellow cornmeal, sugar and salt in processor. Add chilled butter. Using on/off turns, process until mixture resembles coarse meal. Drizzle egg yolk mixture over. Using on/off turns, process until moist clumps form, adding more ice water by teaspoon if dough is dry. Gather dough into ball. Flatten dough into disk; wrap disk in plastic and refrigerate 30 minutes. (Can be prepared 1 day ahead. Keep refrigerated.)

Position rack in bottom third of oven and preheat to 350°. Roll out dough between 2 sheets of waxed paper to 12 inch round. Remove top sheet of waxed paper. Invert dough, paper side up, into 9 inch diameter glass pie dish. Remove waxed paper from dough. Crimp dough edges decoratively.

For filling:

Using electric mixer, beat cream cheese in large bowl until fluffy. Add ½ cup sugar and ½ cup brown sugar and beat until light and fluffy. Beat in eggs and egg yolk one at a time. Add remaining ingredients and beat until well blended. Pour filling into prepared crust.

Bake pie until filling is slightly puffed and just set in center, about 55 minutes. Transfer pie to rack and cool completely. Cover pie and refrigerate until cool, at least 4 hours.

(Can be prepared 1 day ahead. Keep pie refrigerated.)

Serve pie cold.

Wheeler's Steak Marinade
Blue Cheese Grapes
Downeast Pork and Sage Hand Pies
Salad with Creamy Vinaigrette
Green Bean Bundles
Chocolate-Peanut Butter Pound Cake
Sliced Baked Potatoes

WHEELER'S STEAK MARINADE
We love this and the chef too.

1 sirloin steak (about 2 pounds), 2 inches thick
1 bottle Burgundy or Red Table Wine
1 pint milk
1 bottle (20 oz.) teriyaki
1 T. garlic powder
1 T. Seasonall
1 T. course ground pepper
1 T. onion powder
½ t. cumin

Yield: 4-6 servings

Mix all ingredients except steak and wine in large saucepan. Bring to a boil; let cool and add wine. Pour over steak and set in refrigerator for 2-4 hours. Heat skillet to medium heat; add steak and cook for 8 minutes on each side for rare meat. Discard juices.

BLUE CHEESE GRAPES

These sound a bit unusual but are very tasty.

6   oz. cream cheese,
     softened
3   oz. blue cheese
bunch of seedless grapes
1   cup finely chopped pecans

Yield: 8 servings

Mix the softened cream cheese with the blue cheese. Press a thin layer of cheese mixture around each grape and roll the grape in the chopped nuts. Refrigerate until ready to serve.

DOWNEAST PORK AND SAGE HAND PIES

3   T. butter
1   small onion finely
     chopped
2   pounds of lean ground
     pork
2   medium potatoes (boiled,
     peeled and cubed)
2   medium apples, peeled
     and diced
3   T. flour
1   T. brown sugar
½   t. salt
1   t. pepper
4   T. sage
3   ready made pie crusts
2   egg yolks

Yield: about 3 dozen

Melt the butter in a skillet over medium heat. Add the onion and sauté 5 minutes. Add the pork and sauté until well browned (about 10 minutes). Stir in the potatoes and apples. Add the flour until blended and cook 2 minutes longer. Stir in the brown sugar, salt, pepper and sage. Remove from heat.

Preheat the oven to 400°. Cut the pastry into 2 and ½ inch circles. Place a heaping teaspoon of the mixture on one side of each circle. Moisten the edges with water and fold each pastry into a semicircle. Press the edges lightly to seal. (May be made ahead and refrigerated or frozen).

Lightly brush slightly beaten egg yolks over the pies. Place on ungreased baking sheets and bake 20 to 25 minutes.

SALAD WITH CREAMY VINAIGRETTE DRESSING

3   bags/varieties of salad greens
4-6   roma tomatoes, diced
bunch of chives, diced
small can of diced black olives
1   cup almond slivers
6   oz. of feta cheese
3   red bell peppers, julienned
1-2   bunches of asparagus spears, blanched
vinaigrette dressing

On salad plates, arrange each of the above ingredients in the order listed. Top with the dressing. Serve.

Vinaigrette:

2   T. sour cream
4   T. Dijon mustard
2   T. red wine vinegar
1   t. salt
dash pepper
4   T. green onion (tops and bottoms)
1   cup salad oil

Yield: 12-15 servings

Combine all dressing ingredients except salad oil. Mix well. Slowly beat in the oil, continuing to beat until thickened. Pour into tightly covered container and store in refrigerator. This dressing will keep in the refrigerator several weeks.

GREEN BEAN BUNDLES

Our husbands love this vegetable

3-4   cans of whole green beans
or
1   pound of cooked fresh green beans
5-6   strips of bacon

Brown sugar mixture:
½   cup brown sugar
2   oz. melted butter
1   T. Dijon mustard

Yield: 10-12 servings

Cut bacon in half. Wrap each bacon piece around 8 to 10 green beans.

Secure the bundles with a toothpick. Lay them in a glass baking dish. When ready to cook, dollop the brown sugar mixture onto each bundle and cook at 350° for 25 to 30 minutes or until bacon is cooked.

CHOCOLATE PEANUT BUTTER POUND CAKE

Excellent!
Not as hard as it looks and worth the effort

Peanut Butter Mousse:
2   cups powdered sugar, sifted
¾   cups plus 2 T. creamy peanut butter
(do not use freshly ground or old-fashioned style)
6   oz. cream cheese, room temperature
3   T. whipping cream
2   large egg whites

Chocolate Mousse:
1   cup whipping cream
⅓   cup sugar
8   oz. bittersweet or semisweet chocolate, chopped
1 ½   t. instant expresso powder (or instant coffee)
2 ½   T. hot water
3   egg yolks

Chocolate Glaze:
⅔   cup whipping cream
5   T. unsalted butter, diced
5   oz. semisweet chocolate, finely chopped

For garnish:
raspberries
fresh mint sprigs

Yield: 12 servings

For Peanut Butter Mousse:

Line a 6 cup loaf pan with foil. Mix together 1⅓ cups powder sugar, peanut butter and cream cheese in a large bowl until smooth.

Mix in cream. Beat egg whites in a medium bowl until soft peaks form.

Gradually add remaining ⅔ cup powdered sugar and beat until stiff and shiny. Fold whites into peanut butter mixture in two additions.

Tilt prepared pan lengthwise at 45 degree angle. Spoon in peanut butter mousse and smooth top. (Mousse will form a triangle down the length of the pan.) Set pan in freezer, propping to hold it at an angle. Freeze until mousse is firm (about 1 hour).

For Chocolate Mousse:

Heat cream and sugar in heavy small pan over very low heat, stirring just until sugar dissolves. Transfer to medium bowl and refrigerate until well chilled.

(Continued on Next Page)

Meanwhile, melt chocolate in top of double boiler over simmering water, stirring until smooth. Cool 5 minutes. Dissolve expresso powder in hot water in a small bowl. Whisk in yolks. Add mixture to warm chocolate and stir until mixture is smooth and slightly thickened. Let stand until batter is cooled to room temperature, but not set.

Beat chilled cream to soft peaks. Fold cream into chocolate mixture in two additions. Set pan with frozen peanut butter mousse flat onto work surface.

Spoon chocolate mousse over frozen peanut butter mousse. Smooth top.

Cover pan. Freeze until chocolate is firm, about 6 hours or overnight.

For glaze:

Heat cream and butter in medium saucepan over low heat until cream simmers and butter is melted. Turn off heat. Add chocolate and whisk until mixture is smooth. Let cool until thickened but still of pouring consistency, about 1½ hours.

Invert loaf onto cake rack. Remove pan, remove foil. Pour glaze over mousse and smooth all surfaces. Transfer mousse to serving platter. Freeze until glaze is set, about 1 hour. (Can be prepared 1 day ahead.) Wrap loosely when chocolate is frozen solid.

Cut mousse in ½ inch thick slices. Garnish with berries and mint. (Another choice – place each slice on raspberry puree.)

Blessed are those who hunger and thirst for righteousness, for they will be filled.

Matthew 5:6

SLICED BAKED POTATOES

Nice change from baked potatoes
and the presentation is great!

4	medium potatoes
1	t. salt
4	T. melted butter
4	T. chives, chopped
6	T. grated cheddar cheese
2	T. Parmesan cheese

Yield: 4 servings

Peel the potatoes if the skin is tough, otherwise just scrub and rinse them.

Cut potatoes vertically into thin slices, but not all the way through. This will create a "fanned" effect. Use a handle of a spoon laid next to potatoes to prevent knife from cutting all the way through.

Put potatoes in a baking dish. Fan them slightly.

Sprinkle with salt and drizzle with butter. Sprinkle with the chives.

Bake potatoes at 425° for about 50 minutes.

Remove from oven. Sprinkle with cheese.

Bake potatoes for another 10-15 minutes until lightly browned, cheeses are melted and potatoes are soft inside. Check with a fork.

"My idea of heaven is a great big baked potato and someone to share it with."

Oprah Winfrey

Crab Stuffed Mushroom Caps

Mandarin Salad with
Poppy Seed Dressing

Shrimp & Snow Peas

Roasted Prime Rib

Cheesy Anytime Soup

Three Cheese Scalloped Potatoes

Cherry Christmas Tree Cake

CRAB STUFFED
MUSHROOM CAPS

6   lbs. large fresh mushrooms
3   cups onion, finely chopped
½   cup butter or margarine
2   lbs. crabmeat, drained
    and flaked
Juice of 2 lemons
½   cup fresh parsley, chopped
¼   cup capers, drained
2   t. Worcestershire sauce
1   t. salt
½   t. pepper
1   cup mayonnaise
¾   cup dry sherry
½   cup Parmesan cheese,
    grated
1½ cups butter or margarine,
    melted

Yield: about 8 dozen

Clean mushrooms and allow to drain until dry. Remove stems and chop; set aside. Place mushroom caps in a shallow baking dish.

Sauté mushroom stems and onion in ½ cup butter in a skillet until tender. Remove from heat and set aside.

Add sautéed mushrooms and next 7 ingredients; mix well. Stir in mayonnaise and sherry. Spoon mushroom mixture into mushroom caps; sprinkle with cheese. Drizzle remaining butter over mushrooms. Bake at 350° for 20 minutes.

193

MANDARIN SALAD WITH POPPY SEED DRESSING

Great holiday salad

Red leaf lettuce
Romaine
Spinach
Mandarin oranges
Red onion thinly sliced
Avocado slices
Almonds, sliced

Mix fresh red leaf lettuce, romaine and stemmed spinach. Place on salad plates; layer next with mandarin oranges, avocado slices, red onion and sliced almonds. Drizzle with Poppy Seed Dressing.

POPPY SEED DRESSING

Easier and best if made with electric mixer or blender.

1½	cups sugar
2	t. dry mustard
2	t. salt
⅔	cup vinegar
3	T. onion juice
2	cups vegetable oil
3	T. poppy seeds

Mix sugar, mustard, salt and vinegar. Add onion juice and stir it in thoroughly. Add oil slowly, beating constantly and continue to beat until thick. Add poppy seeds and beat for a few minutes. Store in the refrigerator. (The onion juice is obtained by grating a large white onion on the fine side of a grater, or putting it in an electric blender, then strain. If the dressing separates, pour off the clear part and start all over, adding the poppy seed mixture slowly, but it will not separate unless it becomes too hot or cold.)

SHRIMP & SNOW PEAS

4   T. peanut oil
2   lbs. raw shrimp, about 18
    peeled and deveined
2   cups Sherry Vinaigrette
18 snow peas, about one
    pound
Salt, to taste

Yield: 18 portions

Heat half the peanut oil in a small skillet. Sauté half of the shrimp, stirring and tossing frequently until done, about 4 minutes. Shrimp will turn pink and become firm. Do not overcook.

Lift cooked shrimp from skillet with a slotted spoon and transfer them to a small deep bowl just large enough to hold them. Repeat with remaining shrimp.

Pour ½ cup Sherry Vinaigrette over warm shrimp and let stand for one hour.

Meanwhile, trim snow peas and drop them into a kettle of salted boiled water. Let them cook for about 2 minutes; the water need not even return to a boil. Drain immediately and then plunge them into a bowl of ice water. This will stop the cooking process and set the brilliant green color.

When snow peas are completely cool, drain them and pat dry. Split them along their seams, leaving the halves joined at one end.

Remove shrimp, one at a time from the vinaigrette and wrap a snow pea around each shrimp.

Skewer into place with a cocktail pick and arrange on a platter. Cover the platter and refrigerate until serving time.

Drizzle some of the remaining vinaigrette over shrimp just before serving, if desired.

SHERRY VINAIGRETTE

2   T. prepared Dijon-style
    mustard
½   cup sherry wine vinegar
½   t. salt
freshly ground black pepper, to
    taste
3   cups olive oil

Yield: 3½ cups

Whisk the mustard and the sherry vinegar together in a small bowl.

Stir in the salt and black pepper to taste.

Whisking constantly, dribble the olive oil into the vinegar mixture in a slow, steady stream.

Taste, correct seasonings and cover until ready to use.

ROASTED PRIME RIB

The principle of high-heat roasting is to sear the outside of the meat and bring the interior to the desired degree of doneness as rapidly as possible.

Oil the surfaces lacking natural fat coverings. Season lightly with salt and pepper. Place the roast rib side down in a small pan to keep drippings from spreading and charring.

Place the meat in a preheated 500° oven. After 15 minutes, reduce the heat to 350°. Roast until the meat is done, 125° for rare.

CHEESY ANYTIME SOUP

¼	cup butter or margarine
¼	cup plus 2 T. flour
2	(10¾ oz.) cans chicken broth, undiluted
2	cups milk
¼	t. white pepper
2	T. chopped pimento
¼	cup plus 2 T. dry white wine (optional)
¼	t. Worcestershire sauce
¼	t. Tabasco
2	cups (8 oz.) shredded sharp cheddar cheese

Yield: 5 cups

Melt butter in a heavy saucepan over low heat; add flour, stirring until smooth. Cook one minute, stirring constantly. Gradually add broth and milk; cook over medium heat, stirring constantly, until thickened and bubbly. Stir in pepper.

Add next 4 ingredients. Heat to boiling, stirring frequently. Remove from heat; add cheese and stir until cheese melts. Serve immediately.

THREE CHEESES
SCALLOPED POTATOES

¾ cup (packed) grated extra-sharp cheddar cheese
¾ cup crumbled Danish blue cheese
⅓ cup (packed) freshly grated Parmesan
4 pounds potatoes (peeled, and cut into ¼ inch thick rounds)
1½ t. salt
½ t. ground black pepper
¼ cup finely chopped onion
3 T. flour
4 T. butter
3 cups milk

Yields: 12 servings

Preheat oven to 400°. Lightly butter 13 x 9 x 2 inch glass baking dish. Mix cheddar cheese, blue cheese and Parmesan in small bowl.

Arrange half of potatoes in prepared baking dish, overlapping slightly. Sprinkle with ¾ t. salt and ¼ t. pepper. Sprinkle onion over, then flour. Dot with 2 T. butter. Sprinkle half of cheese mixture over. Top with remaining potatoes, ¾ t. salt, ¼ t. pepper and 2 T. butter. Reserve remaining cheese.

Bring milk to simmer in medium saucepan. Pour milk over potatoes (milk will not cover potatoes completely). Cover baking dish tightly with foil. Bake 45 minutes. Uncover dish (liquids in dish may look curdled); sprinkle potatoes with reserved cheese mixture. Bake uncovered until potatoes are tender and cheese is deep golden brown, about 45 minutes longer. (Can be prepared 2 hours ahead. Let stand at room temperature. Cover and rewarm in 375° oven about 20 minutes.)

Remove from oven; let stand 15 minutes before serving.

CHERRY CHRISTMAS TREE CAKE

Makes a huge cake; the kids will love this.

2 pkgs. Duncan Hines Butter Recipe Golden Cake Mix
6 eggs
1 cup softened butter or margarine
1⅓ cups orange juice
Grated peel of 2 oranges
3 21 oz. cans cherry pie filling
2 or 3 cans Duncan Hines Vanilla Frosting (You will need 2 cans to frost cake and 1 can (optional) for decorative frosting)
¾ cup powdered sugar (optional)

Yield: 24 servings

Note: The assembled cake is 9" × 26". If you do not have a platter or tray that size, cover heavy cardboard with aluminum foil. For a smaller party (15 servings), bake and decorate a 9" × 13" cake using half of the ingredients listed above.

Preheat oven to 375°. Grease and flour a 9" × 13" × 2" pan.

Combine in a large bowl: 1 pkg. cake mix, 3 eggs, ½ cup butter, ⅔ cup orange juice. Mix at medium speed for 4 minutes. Stir in grated peel of 1 orange. Pour into prepared pan.

Bake for 35 to 40 minutes. Cake is done when toothpick inserted in center comes out clean. Cool for 15 minutes, then remove cake from pan.

To bake second cake, repeat steps 1 through 4.

Place completely cooled cakes upside-down and end-to-end on platter. Spread 2 cans frosting on top and sides. Draw a tree shape and border in frosting. Optional, mix can of frosting with ¾ cup sifted powdered sugar and pipe decorative border around top and bottom edges of cake.

Place a colander or strainer in a large bowl, pour in cherries and stir to drain (do not rinse). Using a spoon or fork, fill in tree and border with tightly packed rows of cherries.

Seafood Chili Dip
Mini Party Tarts
Seafood Bisque
Brie & Herb Cheese in Pastry
Red Wine Beef Tenderloin Marinade
Salad Greens with Carmelized Pecan
& Feta Cheese
Potato Supreme
Holiday Asparagus
Old Fashioned Whole Wheat Bread
Chocolate Mousse Cake

SEAFOOD CHILI DIP
Wonderful Holiday Dip!

Mix in blender until smooth:

1	bottle Heinz Chili Sauce
1	bunch green onion, chopped
3	ribs celery, chopped
1	green pepper, chopped
3	T. picante sauce
1	T. Worcestershire sauce

Refrigerate 24 hours.

Spread on a large flat plate:

2	8 oz. pkgs. cream cheese, softened

Yield: 8 appetizer servings

Layer on top of the cheese:

½	pound cooked popcorn shrimp or crab meat

Spread sauce over the seafood. Chill.

Serve with assorted crackers.

199

MINI PARTY TARTS

Tart Shells
Combine:

1   3 oz. pkg. cream cheese,
     softened
½   cup
     butter (softened)
1½   cups flour

Yield: 30 tarts

Cream until smooth. Shape into
30 (1") balls. Place each ball in
an ungreased mini muffin pan.
Shape each ball into the shell.

Filling:

Place in paper towels and
squeeze until almost dry: 1-10 oz.

frozen chopped spinach, thawed
and drained.

Then combine with:

1   egg, well beaten
¼   t. salt
⅛   t. pepper
2   T. onion, chopped
1½   cup Romano cheese,
     grated + Reserve ½ cup for
     topping
¼   cup butter, melted

Fill each shell with one heaping
teaspoon of the mixture. Sprinkle
with more Romano Cheese. Bake
at 350° for 30-35 minutes.

SEAFOOD BISQUE

(Superb!)

1   lb. lobster meat
½   lb. Bay shrimp, peeled
     and cleaned
1   carrot, chopped fine, use
     food processor
2   stalks celery, chopped
     fine, use food processor
1   medium onion, chopped
     fine, use food processor
1   T. tarragon
1   T. dill
1½   t. ground cloves
¾   t. lemon pepper
1   pint heavy cream
½   cup brandy

Yield: 6-8 servings

Boil ½ gallon water, add lobster
and shrimp and boil 5 minutes.
Reduce heat, add vegetables
and spices and cook ½ hour.
Make a flour and butter roux to
thicken the soup. Add to mixture
and stir until blended.

Add cream and brandy just
before serving.

BRIE & HERB CHEESES IN PASTRY

1   10" x 9" sheet frozen
puff pastry, thawed
(we recommend
Pepperidge Farm)
1   14 oz. wheel Brie cheese
2   4 oz. packages garlic &
herb semi-soft cheese
1   egg, beaten to blend
1   T. water

Yield: 8 appetizer servings

Lightly flour baking sheet. Place puff pastry on prepared sheet and roll out gently to remove fold lines. Place brie in center of pastry. Spread one package semi-soft cheese on brie. Turn brie over. Spread remaining semi-soft cheese on second side of brie. Bring pastry up around sides and over cheese, wrapping completely and trimming excess pastry. Turn over and place seam side down. Gather pastry scraps, re-roll and cut out to form decorations.

Can be prepared one day ahead. Combine egg and water. Brush over top. Preheat oven to 375°. Bake pastry until golden brown, 30-35 minutes. Let stand ten minutes before serving.

RED WINE BEEF TENDERLOIN MARINADE

1   cup dry red wine
½   cup salad oil
¼   cup soy sauce
¼   cup worcestershire
2   t. parsley
2   t. course ground black
pepper
1   t. Knorr Swiss Aromat
Seasoning for Meat
1   t. sugar
1   clove garlic

Mix all ingredients together in a dish deep enough for marination. Allow tenderloin to marinate 8-24 hours. Sprinkle more Knorr Meat Seasoning & some lemon pepper on meat before grilling. Using a meat thermometer, grill to desired doneness, 125° for rare.

SALAD GREENS WITH CARAMELIZED PECANS AND FETA CHEESE

Salad:
1 head romaine lettuce
1 head red lettuce
6 oz. Feta cheese
½ onion, thinly sliced, (optional)
strawberries, cut into quarter, (optional)

Vinaigrette:
4 T. raspberry vinegar
½ cup olive oil
salt and pepper (to taste)

Caramelized Pecans:
1 T. sugar
½ t. salt
½ t. pepper
1 T. water
⅔ cup pecan halves

Wash lettuce and tear into bite sized pieces. Set aside. Mix together vinaigrette ingredients. In a small saucepan heat the sugar, salt, pepper and water together until bubbly. Add pecans and stir to coat. They will be fragrant. Remove once sugar has caramelized. Cool on wax paper. Toss the lettuce with the pecans, cheese, strawberries and onion.

POTATO SUPREME

5½ cups peeled and sliced (¼") potatoes
1 cup onion, sliced ¼"
1 can cream of mushroom soup
1 can cheddar cheese soup
1 can water or milk
1 stick butter

Yield: 8 servings

Arrange potatoes and onions in layers in a buttered casserole. Mix in a separate bowl: mushroom soup, cheese soup and milk or water. Pour over potatoes. Dot with stick of butter. Bake in a 350° oven for 1½ hours. Serve hot. Can be made ahead and frozen.

HOLIDAY ASPARAGUS

2	10 oz. packages frozen asparagus spears
½	t. salt
¼	t. pepper
1	8 oz. can water chestnuts, sliced and drained
1	4 oz. can sliced mushrooms, drained
1	2 oz. jar diced pimento
1	egg, hard boiled and sliced
2	cups medium white sauce (recipe follows)
1	t. Worcestershire sauce

Yield: 6-8 servings

Preheat oven to 350°. Thaw asparagus and drain well. Cut spears in 1-inch lengths. Place asparagus in a buttered 8 x 12 inch baking dish. Sprinkle with salt and pepper to taste. Layer water chestnuts, mushrooms, pimento and egg over asparagus. To medium white sauce, add Worcestershire, salt and pepper. Pour white sauce over vegetables. Dish may be refrigerated for convenience. Remove from refrigerator and let stand 30 minutes. Bake uncovered for 25 minutes.

WHITE SAUCE

2½	T. butter
2½	T. flour
2½	cups milk
	Salt and Pepper

Melt the butter in a heavy saucepan. Stir in the flour and cook, stirring over low heat for 2-3 minutes. Pour in all of the milk, whisking constantly to blend the mixture smooth. Increase the heat and continue whisking while the sauce comes to a boil. Season with very little salt. Reduce the heat and simmer for at least 45 minutes, stirring occasionally to prevent the sauce from sticking to the bottom of the pan. When the sauce thickens to the desired consistency, add pepper; taste for seasoning and correct if necessary.

"Without bread, without wine, love is nothing."

French Proverb

OLD FASHIONED WHOLE WHEAT BREAD

Use stand mixer and dough hooks.

1   cup milk at 105°
2   T. honey
1   pkg. active dry yeast
2-2¼ cups bread flour
1   cup whole wheat flour
1   t. salt
2   T. butter or margarine
1   egg
Egg wash: (Combine and blend
    well)
1   egg
½   cup milk

Yield: one loaf, 6 servings

Place warm milk and honey in the large mixing bowl and sprinkle yeast over milk. DO NOT STIR. Allow to stand for 10-12 minutes.

When yeast foams add flour, salt, butter or margarine and egg. Turn mixer on to speed (1) for 45 seconds.

Increase speed to (11) and mix 8 minutes.

Place dough in a lightly oiled bowl. Brush oil on top of dough. Allow dough to rise for one hour in warm place.

Punch dough down and roll into a round bail. Cover with a towel and allow to rest for 10-15 minutes.

Roll dough out to one-inch thick and roll up into a loaf shape on a floured board.

Place dough into a buttered 9½" × 5" × 3" loaf pan and brush with egg wash. Cover with a towel.

Allow dough to rise until dough extends 1½" above the pan.

Bake in a preheated 375° oven for 10 minutes and then reduce heat to 350° and bake for 30-35 minutes.

When golden brown and baked, remove from pan and place on a wire rack to cool.

While cooling, brush with melted butter.

CHOCOLATE MOUSSE CAKE

6 sticks unsalted butter
24 oz. semi-sweet chocolate chips
1 dz. eggs, separated
2 pints whipping cream
Chocolate curls
Chocolate wafer crumbs

Yield: 8-10 servings

Melt: 6 sticks unsalted butter and 24 oz. semi-sweet chocolate chips. Cool.

Beat: One dozen egg yolks. Add to the butter and melted chocolate chip mixture.

Beat: One dozen egg whites until stiff.

Fold: Egg whites into chocolate mixture.

Put into a spring form pan and freeze.

Beat: 2 pints whipping cream. DO NOT ADD SUGAR.

Ice cake with whipped cream. Sprinkle chocolate wafer crumbs on top. Add chocolate curls.

He that is of a merry heart hath a continual feast.

Proverbs 15:15

Tangy Stuffed Celery

Spinach-Onion Dip

Italian Sun-dried Tomato Spread

Artichoke Appetizer Squares

Chilled Asparagus Salad with Feta Cheese and Calamata Olives and Balsamic Vinaigrette

Beef Tenderloin stuffed with Wild Rice, Onions, Celery and Fennel

Spaghetti Squash topped with Sweet Potato Mousse

Cranberry Upside-Down Cake

This is a wonderful holiday menu and the appetizers are especially good.

"Roast beef medium is not a food. It is a philosophy."

Edna Ferber

TANGY STUFFED CELERY

1 pkg. (8 oz.) light cream cheese, softened
1 pkg. (4 oz.) blue cheese
½ cup grated onion
1 T. Dijon mustard
1 T. prepared horseradish
1 t. Worcestershire sauce
Celery ribs, trimmed and cut into 2-inch pieces

Yield: 2 dozen

In a medium mixing bowl, combine cream cheese and blue cheese; mix until well blended. Add grated onion, mustard, horseradish and Worcestershire sauce. Beat until smooth.

Put cheese mixture in a pastry bag fitted with a large leaf tip; pipe mixture into celery sticks (or use a spoon to fill the celery).

SPINACH — ONION DIP

1 pkg. (10 oz.) frozen spinach, thawed
1 cup low-fat cottage cheese
1 T. lemon juice
½ cup plain yogurt or light sour cream
½ cup chopped fresh parsley
¼ cup chopped green onions (green and white parts)
½ t. hot pepper sauce
Pita Bread Chips

Yield: 6-8 servings

Drain spinach, squeezing out as much moisture as possible. In a food processor or electric blender, combine cottage cheese and lemon juice; process until smooth. Add spinach, yogurt, parsley, green onions and hot pepper sauce; process until just mixed. Refrigerate, covered, at least 4 hours. Serve with pita chips or other dippers.

ITALIAN SUN-DRIED TOMATO SPREAD

1   cup sun-dried tomates
Boiling water
5   T. olive oil
2   T. red wine vinegar
1   T. capers
2   cloves garlic, minced
2   t. Italian seasoning
1   t. salt
Melba toast and ricotta cheese
    to serve

Yield: 2 dozen

Place tomatoes in a small bowl and add boiling water to cover. Allow to sit 15 minutes; drain.

Place tomatoes in a food processor and puree. Add oil, vinegar, capers, garlic, Italian seasoning, and salt. Process until well blended and mixture is still slightly coarse. Adjust seasonings, if desired. Store in a jar in refrigerator until ready to serve.

To serve spread Melba toast with ricotta cheese and top with sun-dried tomato spread.

ARTICHOKE APPETIZER SQUARES

1   8 oz. can Pillsbury
    Crescent dinner rolls
2   T. grated Parmesan cheese
2   3 oz. pkg. cream cheese,
    softened
½   cup dairy sour cream
½   t. dried dill weed
¼   t. seasoned salt
1   egg
⅓   cup chopped green onions
1   14 oz. can artichoke
    hearts, drained, chopped
1   2 oz. jar diced pimento,
    drained

Yield: 24 appetizers

Heat oven to 375°. Unroll dough into long rectangle in ungreased 13 x 9 inch pan; seal perforations. Press over bottom and ½ inch up sides to form crust. Sprinkle with Parmesan cheese. Bake at 375° for 5 minutes.

In small bowl, beat cream cheese until smooth. Add sour cream, dill weed, salt and egg; blend well. Spread over partially baked crust. Top with remaining ingredients. Return to oven and bake an additional 13 to 19 minutes or until edges are deep golden brown and center is set. To serve, cut into squares. Serve warm or cold. Store in refrigerator.

CHILLED ASPARAGUS SALAD WITH FETA CHEESE AND CALAMATA OLIVES

6	oz. sundried tomatoes, julienned
3	oz. feta cheese crumbs
3	oz. calamata olives
36	asparagus spears, blanched
6	oz. baby greens
6	radicchio leaf cups
12	Belgium endive leaves
3	oz. balsamic vinaigrette (recipe follows)
3	oz. fresh chives, chopped
1	t. black pepper, coarsely ground

Yield: 6 servings

Combine the julienned tomatoes, feta cheese crumbs and the calamata olives in a small bowl. To assemble salad, place 6 asparagus spears on a salad plate with tips fanned out, pointing towards the front of the plate. Place 1 oz. of the baby greens inside a radicchio leaf cup and set it at the base of the fanned asparagus. Place 2 endive leaves on either side of radicchio leaf cup. Spoon 2 oz. of the olive mixture in between asparagus spears. Dress with balsamic vinaigrette. Garnish with fresh chives and coarsely ground black pepper. Repeat procedure with remaining plates.

BALSAMIC VINAIGRETTE

¼	cup balsamic vinegar
1	t. lemon juice, freshly squeezed
1	t. red wine vinegar
¼	cup white vinegar
1	t. shallot, finely chopped
½	t. garlic, finely chopped
1	t. Dijon mustard
¼	t. sugar
⅛	cup olive oil
¼	cup corn oil
1	T. fresh thyme, stems removed
1	T. fresh basil, chopped
1	T. fresh parsley, chopped
1	T. fresh chives, chopped
	Salt and pepper

In a mixing bowl, combine all of the ingredients by hand except the oils, herbs and salt and pepper. Let the mixture sit for 5 minutes. Then add the olive oil slowly in a stream, followed by the corn oil. Add the herbs and season with salt and pepper to taste.

BEEF TENDERLOIN STUFFED WITH WILD RICE, ONIONS, CELERY AND FENNEL

Beef Tenderloin (¾ pound per person) *Have butcher butterfly meat
1   onion, chopped fine
2   ribs celery, chopped
1   T. fennel
¼   cup olive oil
2   cups Italian breadcrumbs

Sauté onion, celery and fennel in oil until soft. Open butterflied tenderloin and fill with veggies. Close and tie with kitchen twine. Pat olive oil all over and roll in Italian breadcrumbs. Bake at 350° for one hour.

SPAGHETTI SQUASH TOPPED WITH SWEET POTATO MOUSSE

5   spaghetti squash
3   medium sweet potatoes, peeled
2   t. lemon zest
1   T. cinnamon
½   T. nutmeg
Salt and pepper to taste

Yields: 6-8 portions

Cut spaghetti squash in halves and place on baking sheet with ¼ inch water. Sprinkle with salt and pepper. Bake at 350° for one hour. Rake out squash and season again. Place in serving dish. For the sweet potato mousse, boil the sweet potatoes. Drain and mash. Mix in lemon zest, cinnamon and nutmeg. Put in piping bag and pipe on top of spaghetti squash. Serve warm.

CRANBERRY
UPSIDE-DOWN CAKE

12 T. unsalted butter, at room temperature, plus more for pan
2¾ cups fresh or defrosted frozen cranberries
9 T. maple syrup
½ t. ground cinnamon
¾ cup all-purpose flour, plus more for pan
1 t. baking powder
¼ t. salt
6 T. yellow cornmeal, preferably coarse
¼ cup almond paste
¾ cup plus 2 T. sugar
3 large eggs, separated
¼ t. vanilla extract
¼ t. almond extract
½ cup milk

Yield: 10 servings

Butter and flour an 9-inch round cake pan; set aside. In a large skillet, heat 6 T. butter over medium heat until it melts. Add cranberries and cook until shiny, 2 to 3 minutes.

Add maple syrup and cinnamon. Cook, stirring frequently, until cranberries soften but still hold their shape, about 5 minutes.

Remove cranberries with a slotted spoon and transfer to a baking sheet to cool slightly. Set skillet with syrup aside.

Arrange cranberries in the prepared pan.

Return skillet with syrup to medium heat until syrup boils, 3 to 4 minutes; do not overcook. Immediately pour syrup over cranberries and let cool, about 10 minutes.

Place rack in center of oven and heat to 350°. Sift together flour, baking powder, and salt. Mix in cornmeal with a fork.

Place remaining 6 T. butter in an electric mixer bowl. Crumble in almond paste and, using the paddle, beat on medium speed until well combined, about 30 seconds. Gradually add ¾ cup sugar and beat until creamy. Add egg yolks and beat until well combined. Beat in vanilla and almond extracts. Add flour mixture alternately with milk in two batches. Set aside.

In a clean bowl, use the whisk attachment to beat egg whites until foamy. Slowly add remaining 2 T. sugar; beat until soft peaks form. Whisk a third of the whites into batter, then fold in remaining whites.

Spread batter over cranberries and bake for 45 minutes, or until a toothpick inserted in center comes out clean. Let cool in pan 2 hours before inverting onto a serving plate.

Caramelized Asparagus

Marinated Shrimp

Spinach-Wrapped Chicken with Oriental Dip

Sage Butter

Spinach Stuffed Pork Roast

Praline Sweet Potatoes

Pecan Pie Cake

CARMELIZED ASPARAGUS

1	bunch asparagus
2	T. olive oil
2-4	cloves minced garlic
¼	cup honey

Yield: 4 servings

Blanch asparagus, set aside.

In a hot skillet, heat olive oil and add minced garlic. (The more the better.) While stirfrying, add honey to caramelize. Coat asparagus with mixture and serve hot.

MARINATED SHRIMP

This recipe will have your guest coming back for more –
it is so good!

2	pounds raw, peeled and deveined shrimp, (41 count or larger) leave the tails on!
2	medium white or purple (or mixture) onions, sliced into rings
1	cup vegetable oil
1½	cups white vinegar
½	cup sugar
1½	t. salt
1½	t. celery seed
4	T. capers with juice

Yield: 10 servings of 4 shrimp each

Place shrimp in boiling salted water, reduce heat and simmer for 3-5 minutes. Shrimp are done when pink and tender. Drain; rinse with cold water; chill.

Make alternate layers of shrimp and onion rings in a sealable container. Mix remaining ingredients and pour over shrimp and onions. Seal and place in refrigerator for **at least** 6 hours, shaking and/or inverting several times. Drain and serve.

Note: when deveining shrimp, make a cut partially through the shrimp. This will allow the flavors to penetrate the shrimp better. Also, if possible, prepare the shrimp the night before you want to serve them. They will be more flavorful if marinated a full day.

SPINACH-WRAPPED CHICKEN WITH ORIENTAL DIP

This is an awesome appetizer and
one you will surely want to try.

2   lbs. chicken tenders
1   14-oz. can chicken broth
¼   cup soy sauce
1   T. Worchestershire sauce
2   lbs. fresh spinach

Dip:
½   cup sour cream
1   t. toasted sesame seed
2   t. soy sauce
¼   t. ground ginger
1   t. Worchestershire sauce
¼   t. garlic powder

Yield: 50-60 pieces

Combine ingredients for dip and refrigerate.

Simmer the chicken with broth, soy sauce and worchestershire sauce until fork tender. Remove chicken from broth and cool. Cut meat into 1 inch chunks.

Wash spinach thoroughly, removing stems and place leaves in a colander. Bring 3 quarts of water to a boil and pour over spinach. Drain spinach thoroughly and set aside to cool.

To assemble, place a chunk of chicken at a stem end of spinach leaf and carefully roll the spinach around the chicken. Secure spinach with a wooden pick. (Larger leaves of spinach make the task easier.)

Refrigerate until chilled or overnight. Serve with dip. Makes 50-60 pieces.

SAGE BUTTER

For your favorite bread

1   cup butter, softened
1   t. finely snipped fresh sage
        or 1 t. dried sage
fresh herb springs (optional)

In a small bowl combine butter with fresh or dried sage. Shape into butter molds. Chill in the refrigerator at least 2 hours or overnight.

214

SPINACH-STUFFED PORK ROAST

¼ cup chopped fresh mushrooms
¼ cup chopped onion
1 T. vegetable oil
1 pkg. (10 oz.) frozen chopped spinach, thawed and well drained
1 cup soft bread crumbs
½ t. salt
½ t. pepper
¼ t. garlic powder
¼ t. rubbed sage
1 boneless pork loin roast (4 to 5 lbs.), tied

Yield: 8 servings

In a skillet, sauté mushrooms and onion in oil until tender. Stir in spinach, breadcrumbs, salt, pepper, garlic powder and sage. Untie pork roast and separate the loins. Spread stuffing over one loin to within 1 inch of the edges. Top with the remaining loin; retie securely with heavy string. Place in an ungreased shallow baking pan. Bake, uncovered, at 325° for 2½ hours or until a meat thermometer reads 160-170°. Let stand for 15 minutes before slicing.

PRALINE SWEET POTATOES

You will love these sweet potatoes. A group favorite.

3 cups cooked and mashed sweet potatoes
1 cup sugar
2 eggs
1 t. vanilla
⅓ cup milk
½ cup butter or margarine
1 cup brown sugar

⅓ cup flour
⅓ cup butter
1 cup chopped pecans

Yield: 8-10 servings

Mix butter, flour and pecans to form a crumble topping. Sprinkle over the sweet potatoes. Bake at 350° for 30 minutes. Can be made ahead and frozen.

Topping should be added just before baking.

Place the sweet potatoes in a large mixing bowl with all the ingredients above and beat until smooth. (A mixer works best.) Spoon into a 9 x 13 baking dish and top with the following mixture:

PECAN PIE CAKE

Absolutely divine! Serve warm and they won't stop raving.

3	cups finely chopped pecans, toasted and divided
½	cup butter or margarine, softened
½	cup shortening
2	cups sugar
5	large eggs, separated
1	T. vanilla extract
2	cups all-purpose flour
1	t. baking soda
1	cup buttermilk
¾	cup dark corn syrup
1	recipe Pecan Pie Filling (recipe follows)
1	recipe pastry Garnish (optional) recipe follows

Yield: 12 servings

1-3 layer cake

Sprinkle 2 cups pecans evenly into 3 generously buttered 9 inch round cakepans: shake to coat bottoms and sides of pans.

Beat ½ cup butter and shortening at medium speed with an electric mixer until fluffy; gradually add sugar, beating well. Add egg yolks, 1 at a time, beating until blended after each addition. Stir in vanilla.

Add flour and baking soda to butter mixture alternately with buttermilk, beginning and ending with flour. Beat at low speed until blended after each addition. Stir in remaining 1 cup finely chopped pecans.

Beat egg whites at medium speed until stiff peaks form; fold one-third of egg whites into batter. Fold in remaining egg whites. (Do not over mix.) Pour batter into prepared pans.

Bake at 350° for 25 minutes or until done. Cool in pans on wire racks 10 minutes. Invert layers onto wax paper-lined wire racks. Brush tops and sides of layers with corn syrup and cool completely.

Spread half of Pecan Pie Filling on 1 layer, pecan side up. Place second layer, pecan side up, on filling; spread with remaining filling. Top with remaining layer, pecan side up.

Arrange Pastry Garnish on and around cake, if desired.

(Continued on Next Page)

PECAN PIE FILLING

½   cup firmly packed dark
    brown sugar
¾   cup dark corn syrup
⅓   cup cornstarch
4   egg yolks
1½ cups half-and-half
⅛   t. salt
3   T. butter or margarine
1   t. vanilla extract

Yields about 3 cups

Whisk together first 6 ingredients in a heavy 3-quart saucepan until smooth. Bring mixture to a boil over medium heat, whisking constantly; boil 1 minute or until thickened. Remove from heat; whisk in butter and vanilla extract. Place a sheet of wax paper directly on surface of mixture to prevent a film from forming and chill 4 hours.

Note: To chill filling quickly, pour filling into a bowl. Place bowl in a larger bowl filled with ice. Whisk constantly until cool (about 15 minutes).

PASTRY GARNISH

1   15 oz. package
    refrigerated piecrusts
1   large egg
1   T. water
24 pecan halves

Yields 16-20 pastry leaves and 12 pecan pastries.

Unfold piecrusts, and press out fold lines. Cut 8 to 10 leaves from each piecrust with a 3 inch leaf-shaped cutter, and mark leaf veins using tip of a knife. Reserve pastry trimmings. Whisk together egg and 1 T. water and brush on pastry leaves.

Crumple 10 to 12 small aluminum foil pieces into ½ inch balls. Coat with vegetable cooking spray and place on a lightly greased baking sheet. Drape a pastry leaf over each ball (this gives the leafs movement and variety); place remaining pastry leaves on baking sheet.

Bake at 425° for 6 to 8 minutes or until golden brown. Cool on a wire rack 10 minutes. Gently remove foil from leaves.

Pinch 12 pea-size pieces from pastry trimmings. Place between pecan halves, forming sandwiches. Cut remaining pastry into 2 inch pieces; wrap around pecan sandwiches, leaving jagged edges to resemble half-shelled pecans. Brush with egg mixture. Place on baking sheet.

Bake at 350° for 10 minutes or until golden. Cool on wire rack.

Spinach-Cheese Puffs

Spinach Salad

Beef Tenderloin Bearnaise

Tortellini Tapas with Spicy Ranch Dip

*Roasted Asparagus with
Red Pepper Sauce*

Pistachio Risotto with Saffron

*French Bread Pudding with
Whisky Sauce*

SPINACH-CHEESE PUFFS

1 pkg. Stouffers frozen
   spinach souffle
6 medium fresh mushrooms,
   sliced
2 pkgs. Crescent Rolls
   (refrigerated kind)
½-¾ cup grated sharp cheddar
   cheese
2 t. onion flakes
¼ cup seasoned bread
   crumbs
Salt to taste

Yield: 24 appetizers

Cook frozen spinach souffle as package directs. (Can be microwaved). Wash and dry fresh mushrooms, then slice into thin slices, being certain to remove stems. While spinach is still hot, mix in cheese, onion flakes, bread crumbs and salt. Open cans of crescent rolls. Dough comes out of can to form a rectangle. Pinch perforated dough together to form 4 large rectangles, per can. Then cut into thirds. On top of each piece of dough place thin mushroom slice, small portion of souffle mixture and extra cheese if desired. Roll up dough and place on cookie sheet. Place in a 400° oven for 15-20 minutes or until lightly browned. Serve warm.

SPINACH SALAD

1	large package baby spinach
1	(4 oz.) pkg. sliced almonds, toasted
3-4	cans mandarin oranges, drained
6	oz. fresh grated parmesan cheese

Dressing:

2	cups oil
1	cup Heinz red wine vinegar
1	cup sugar
½	t. dry mustard
½	t. worcestershire sauce
½	t. onion powder

Yield: 10 servings

Shake. (Don't use all dressing for this amount of salad. Refrigerate remaining. Use dressing sparingly.) Toss dressing with salad ingredients.

BEEF TENDERLOIN BEARNAISE

4	pound beef tenderloin
4	T. butter (melted)

Brush the tenderloin with the melted butter. Place on rack in shallow roasting pan. Roast uncovered in 425° oven 45 to 60 minutes. Serve with Bearnaise Sauce.

Bearnaise Sauce:

2	egg yolks
3	T. lemon juice
½	cup firm butter
2	T. white wine or 1 T. white wine vinegar
1	T. finely chopped onion
1	t. dried tarragon leaves
½	t. dried chervil leaves

Yield: 12 servings

Stir egg yolks and lemon juice vigorously in 1 quart saucepan with wooden spoon. Add half of the butter. Heat over very low heat, stirring constantly, until butter is melted. Add remaining butter. Cook, stirring vigorously, until butter is melted and sauce thickens. (Be sure butter melts slowly because this gives eggs time to cook and thicken sauce without curdling.) Stir in remaining ingredients.

219

TORTELLINI TAPAS WITH SPICY RANCH DIP

1   (9-oz.) package
    refrigerated cheese-filled
    tortellini
1   (16-oz.) bottle Ranch-style
    dressing with peppercorns,
    divided*
2   large eggs
2   cups fine, dry
    breadcrumbs
¾   cup mild chunky salsa
¼   cup chopped fresh cilantro
2   cups vegetable oil
Garnish: fresh cilantro sprigs

Yield: 8 appetizer servings

Cook tortellini according to package directions; drain and cool.

Whisk together 1 cup dressing and eggs in a large bowl until blended. Add tortellini, and let stand 10 minutes. Drain and dredge in breadcrumbs; place on a baking sheet. Chill at least 1 hour.

Stir together remaining dressing, salsa, and cilantro; chill.

Pour oil into a Dutch oven; heat to 375°. Fry tortellini, in batches, until golden brown. Drain on paper towels. Serve with dip; garnish, if desired.

* 1 (16-oz) bottle Ranch-style dressing plus ½ t. cracked black pepper may be substituted.

Note: To make ahead, fry tortellini according to directions; drain and place on a baking sheet. Keep warm in a 200° oven for 2 hours.

ROASTED ASPARAGUS WITH RED PEPPER SAUCE

3   T. olive oil
2   T. balsamic vinegar
1   T. teriyaki sauce
1   T. dried basil
½   t. salt
½   t. pepper
¼   t. dry mustard
¼   t. ground nutmeg
1½   lbs. fresh asparagus, trimmed*
Red Pepper Sauce (recipe follows)

Yield: 6 servings

Stir together oil and next 7 ingredients in an 11 × 7 inch baking dish. Add asparagus, and toss to coat.

Bake, covered, at 375° for 35 minutes, turning asparagus once. Remove with a slotted spoon, and serve with Red Pepper Sauce.

*2 (10-oz.) pkgs. frozen asparagus, thawed, may be substituted.

RED PEPPER SAUCE

1   (7-oz.) jar roasted sweet red peppers, drained and sliced
½   small onion, chopped
1   garlic clove, minced
2   T. olive oil
1   T. balsamic vinegar
1   T. orange marmalade
1   T. teriyaki sauce
¼   t. dry mustard
¼   t. ground nutmeg
⅛   t. dried crushed red pepper
¼   cup mayonnaise

Yield: 1¼ cups

Sauté first 3 ingredients in hot oil in a large skillet over medium-high heat 2 minutes. Add vinegar and next 5 ingredients, and cook 3 minutes. Remove from heat, and stir in mayonnaise.

PISTACHIO RISOTTO WITH SAFFRON

Well worth the time.

¼ cup unsalted butter
1 medium-size yellow onion, chopped
1 t. saffron threads (can use Arborio rice with saffron instead)
1¾ cups uncooked Arborio rice
1 cup dry white vermouth*
5 cups chicken broth
1 cup freshly grated Parmesan cheese
3 T. coarsely chopped pistachios

Yield: 8 cups

Melt butter in a large skillet over medium-high heat; add onion, and sauté 5 minutes. Add saffron, and sauté 1 minute.

Add rice, and cook, stirring constantly, 2 minutes. Reduce heat to medium; add vermouth and 2 cups *heated* broth. Cook, stirring constantly, until liquid is absorbed.

Repeat procedure with remaining broth, ½ cup at a time. (Cooking time is 30 to 45 minutes.)

Remove from heat, stir in cheese and pistachios.

*1 cup chicken broth may be substituted for vermouth.

FRENCH BREAD PUDDING WITH WHISKEY SAUCE

You and your company will love this bread pudding.

1	cup sugar
1	stick butter, softened
5	eggs, beaten
1	pint heavy cream
Dash of cinnamon	
1	T. vanilla extract
¼	cup raisins (optional)
12	slices, each 1 inch thick, of fresh or stale bread with crust removed

Preheat oven to 350°.

In a large bowl, cream together the sugar and butter. Add eggs, cream, cinnamon, vanilla, and raisins, mixing well. Pour into a 9-inch square pan, 1¾ inches deep.

Arrange bread slices flat in the egg mixture and let stand for 5 min. to soak up some of the liquid. Turn bread over and let stand for 10 minutes longer. Then push bread down so that most of it is covered by the egg mixture. Do not break the bread.

Set pan in a larger pan filled with water to ½ inch from top. Cover with aluminum foil. Bake for 45 to 50 minutes, uncovering pudding for the last 10 minutes to brown the top. When done, the custard should still be soft, not firm.

Whiskey Sauce

1	cup sugar
1	cup heavy cream
Dash of cinnamon	
1	T. unsalted butter
½	t. cornstarch
1	T. bourbon
¼	cup additional water

Yield: 8-10 servings

To make the sauce, while pudding is baking, combine in a sauce pan the sugar, cream, cinnamon and butter. Bring to a boil. Add in the cornstarch mixed with the ¼ cup water and cook, stirring until sauce is clear. Remove from heat and stir in whiskey.

To serve: remove bread pudding from oven and serve immediately with the sauce in a separate bowl.

Holiday House Salad
Crab Puffs
Sun-Dried Tomato Cheesecake Squares
Baked Ham and Glazed Apricots
Spinach and Ricotta Stuffed Tomatoes
Potato and Yam au Gratin
Baked Zucchini Fans
Caramel-Filled Butter Pecan Cake
Holiday Wassail

HOLIDAY HOUSE SALAD

2   heads of leaf lettuce
    (curly, one purple)
1   Boston or bib lettuce
½   cup of grated carrots (2)
½   cup of grated Parmesan
    cheese
¼   cup toasted sesame seeds
1   cup toasted sunflower
    seeds (or roasted)
1   cup roasted pumpkin seed
1   cup toasted almonds
    (sliced)

Yield: 8-10 servings

Tear cleaned lettuce and mix the lettuces. Add seeds, carrots, and cheese. Mix into lettuce.

Dressing:

⅓   cup Regina white wine
    vinegar
⅔   cup vegetable oil
pinch of sweet & low

Mix 3 ingredients together. Mix well and pour over salad.

CRAB PUFFS

Yummy appetizer!

1	6 oz. can crabmeat, drained and flaked
½	cup shredded sharp cheddar cheese
3	green onions, chopped
1	t. dry mustard
1	t. Worcestershire sauce
1	cup water
½	cup butter or margarine
¼	t. salt
1	cup all-purpose flour
4	eggs

Yield: 4½ dozen

Combine first 5 ingredients, stirring well; set aside.

Combine water, butter, and salt in a medium saucepan; bring mixture to a boil. Reduce heat to low; add flour, and stir vigorously until mixture leaves sides of pan and forms a smooth ball. Remove saucepan from heat, and allow mixture to cool slightly.

Add eggs, one at a time, beating with a wooden spoon after each addition; beat until batter is smooth. Add crab mixture; stir well.

Drop batter by heaping teaspoonfuls onto ungreased baking sheets. Bake at 400° for 15 minutes; reduce heat to 350°, and bake an additional 10 minutes. Serve puffs warm.

To freeze before baking, cover baking sheets with foil before dropping batter onto them. Place unbaked puffs on baking sheets in freezer until hard. Remove from sheets, and store in an airtight container in freezer. To serve, remove from freezer, and bake, unthawed, at 375° for 35 minutes.

To freeze after baking, place crab puffs in an airtight container in freezer. To serve, remove from freezer, let thaw completely, and bake at 350° for 8 to 10 minutes.

SUN-DRIED TOMATO CHEESECAKE SQUARES

This is always a hit at parties!

CRUST:
1¼   cups all purpose flour
6   T. chilled unsalted butter,
      cut into pieces
1   large egg

FILLING:
½   cup drained oil-packed
      sun-dried tomatoes
      (1 T. oil reserved)
6   garlic cloves
2   t. chopped fresh oregano
      or ½ t. dried, crumbled
3   large eggs
2   8 oz. pkgs cream cheese,
      cut into pieces, room
      temperature
1   cup sour cream
½   cup finely chopped green
      onions
Arugula or Boston lettuce
      leaves (optional)

Yield: 12 servings

FOR CRUST:
Preheat oven to 350°. Blend flour with butter in processor using on/off turns until mixture resembles coarse meal. Add egg and blend just until dough begins to clump together. Press dough onto bottom of 9 x 13 baking dish (dough will be thin). Bake crust until light golden brown, about 10 minutes (crust may crack). Cool. Maintain oven temperature.

FOR FILLING:
Finely chop sun-dried tomatoes with 1 T. reserved oil, garlic cloves and oregano in processor. Blend in eggs. Add cream cheese and blend until smooth. Add sour cream and blend until combined. Transfer tomato filling to bowl. Mix in finely chopped green onions. Season filling with salt and pepper.

Pour filling into crust. Bake until filling puffs and is light brown, about 20 minutes. Cool to room temperature. Line platter with Arugula or Boston lettuce leaves. Cut tomato cheesecake into squares. Arrange squares on platter and serve.

BAKED HAM AND GLAZED APRICOTS

1   ready to eat ham with bone (6 to 8 pounds)
whole cloves (to cover surface of ham)
¼   cup prepared Dijon-style mustard
½   cup brown sugar
2   cups apple juice
½   pound dried apricots
½   cup white wine

Yields: 10 to 12 portions

Preheat oven to 350°. Peel skin from the ham and trim fat, leaving about a ¼ inch layer to protect meat. With a sharp knife score fat in a diamond pattern. Set ham in a shallow baking pan, insert a whole clove in the crossed point of each diamond, and pat the mustard over the top and sides. Sprinkle the top with the brown sugar and pour the apple juice into the bottom of the pan. Bake the ham for 1½ hours, basting frequently.

Meanwhile, combine the apricots and the wine in a small saucepan. Bring this to a boil, cover and remove from the heat.

At 30 minutes from the end of baking time, add apricots and their liquid to the roasting pan and continue to bake and baste the ham.

Transfer ham to a large platter. Decorate the top with apricots. Serve.

SPINACH AND RICOTTA STUFFED TOMATOES

8   ripe red tomatoes
salt
3   T. quality olive oil
1   cup finely chopped
     yellow onions
10   oz. frozen spinach,
     defrosted, drained, and
     squeezed dry
salt and freshly ground black
     pepper, to taste
1   cup ricotta cheese
2   egg yolks
¼   cup grated imported
     Parmesan cheese, plus
     additional cheese to top
     tomatoes
½   cup chopped Italian
     parsley

Yield: 8 servings

Wash and dry the tomatoes and cut off their tops. With a metal measuring tablespoon or the handle end of a small spoon, scrap out seeds and partitions, being careful not to pierce the sides of tomatoes. Salt the cavities and set tomatoes upside down on a paper towel to drain for 30 minutes.

Heat the olive oil in a skillet, add the onions and cook, covered, over low heat until tender and lightly colored, about 25 minutes.

Chop the spinach and add it to the skillet. Combine onions and spinach thoroughly, season to taste with salt, pepper and cover. Cook over low heat, stirring occasionally, for 10 minutes. Do not let the mixture scorch.

Beat ricotta and egg yolks together thoroughly in a mixing bowl. Add spinach mixture, ¼ cup of the Parmesan and the parsley, and season to taste with salt and pepper.

Gently blot tomato cavities dry with a paper towel and spoon an equal share of the spinach mixture into each one. Top each tomato with a sprinkle of additional Parmesan.

Arrange tomatoes in a shallow baking dish and set in the upper third of a preheated 350° oven. Bake until tops are well browned and filling is hot and bubbly, about 20 minutes. Serve immediately.

POTATO AND YAM AU GRATIN

Nice variety and pretty too.

1 t. butter
¾ cup whipping cream
¾ t. salt
¾ t. white pepper
dash nutmeg (fresh best)
1 pound potatoes
1 pound yams (same *as* sweet potatoes)
⅓ cup fresh chives
½-1 cup fresh Parmesan

Yield: 12-15 servings

Pre-heat oven to 350°. Butter 9 x 13 dish. In a bowl, mix cream, salt, pepper and nutmeg.

Peel potatoes and yams, slice very thin (processor does well).

Place potatoes in ice water to avoid discoloring. Dry potatoes.

To assemble:

layer of potatoes (overlap)
layer of yams (overlap)
drizzle cream mixture
sprinkle Parmesan
repeat
top with cheese

Cover with foil. Cook 35 minutes then remove foil and cook 35 to 40 minutes more.

BAKED ZUCCHINI FANS

3 T. finely chopped onion
2 small cloves garlic, crushed
¼ cup olive oil, divided
3 T. soft breadcrumbs
12 small zucchini
¼ cup grated Parmesan cheese

Yield: 12 servings

Sauté onion and crushed garlic in 2 T. olive oil until tender. Remove from heat; stir in breadcrumbs. Set aside.

Cut each zucchini into 4 lengthwise slices leaving slices attached on stem end. Fan slices out, and place in 15 x 10 x 1 inch jellyroll pans; brush zucchini fans lightly with remaining 2 tablespoons olive oil.

Sprinkle each zucchini fan lightly with ½ teaspoon breadcrumb mixture and 1 teaspoon Parmesan cheese. Bake at 350° for 15 to 20 minutes or until crisp-tender.

CARAMEL–FILLED BUTTER PECAN CAKE

1	cup shortening
2	cups sugar
4	eggs
3	cups sifted cake flour
2½	t. baking powder
½	t. salt
1	cup milk
1	t. almond extract
1	t. vanilla extract

Caramel Filling (recipe follows)
Butter Cream Frosting
    (recipe follows)

1	cup chopped pecans

Pecan halves

Cream shortening in a large mixing bowl; gradually add sugar, beating well at medium speed. Add eggs, one at a time, beating well after each addition.

Combine flour, baking powder, and salt; add to creamed mixture alternately with milk, beginning and ending with flour mixture. Mix after each addition. Stir in flavorings.

Grease three 9-inch round cake pans, and line with wax paper; grease wax paper. Pour batter into prepared pans; bake at 375° for 22 to 25 minutes or until a wooden pick inserted in center comes out clean. Cool in pans 10 minutes; remove from pans, and let cool completely on wire racks. Spread Caramel Filling between layers and on top of cake. Spread Butter Cream Frosting on sides of cake. Press chopped pecans into frosting on sides of cake. Garnish top with pecan halves.

(Continued on Next Page)

CARAMEL FILLING

3 cups sugar, divided
¾ cup milk
1 egg, beaten
Pinch of salt
½ cup butter or margarine, cut up

Sprinkle ½ cup sugar in a large heavy saucepan. Place over medium heat and cook, stirring constantly, until sugar melts and syrup is light golden brown.

Combine remaining 2½ cups sugar, milk, egg, and salt, stirring well; stir in butter. Stir butter mixture into hot caramelized sugar. (The mixture will tend to lump, becoming smooth with further cooking.)

Cook over medium heat, stirring frequently, until a candy thermometer registers 230° (15 to 20 minutes). Cool 5 minutes. Beat with a wooden spoon to almost spreading consistency.

BUTTER CREAM FROSTING

⅓ cup butter or margarine, softened
3 cups sifted powdered sugar
2-3 T. half-and-half
½ t. vanilla extract

Yield: 12-15 servings

1-3 layered cake

Cream butter at medium speed with electric mixer; gradually add sugar alternately with half-and-half, beating until light and fluffy. Stir in vanilla.

HOLIDAY WASSAIL

6 cups apple cider
2½ cups apricot nectar
2 cups unsweetened pineapple juice
1 cup orange juice
1 t. whole cloves
4 whole allspice
3 sticks cinnamon

Yield: about 3 quarts

Combine all ingredients in a Dutch over; bring to a boil. Reduce heat, and simmer 15 minutes. Strain and discard spices. Serve hot.

FAB FIVE FOOTNOTES

Whet the appetite don't satisfy it. Plan appetizers to complement the menu.

One teaspoon of butter should be added to chocolate when melting it to be used in an icing recipe.

For easier slicing and to let juices receed into the meat, let cooked roasts and steaks stand at room temperature for 10 minutes before carving.

Bake pies in the lower third of the oven for a crisp bottom crust and to keep the rim or top crust from browning.

Did you know? Keep your shelled nuts in plastic bags in the freezer to prevent their becoming rancid.

Nuts stored in the freezer stay fresher longer. Frozen, however, do take longer to toast than the thawed version. Don't turn up the heat, just bake an extra five minutes.

When baking bread, measure all ingredients carefully, including salt. Salt plays a definite role in developing the dough's flavor and helps control the rising rate of the dough.

Don't throw out shrimp shells, place the washed shells in a saucepan, cover with water and bring to a boil. Reduce heat; cover and simmer 30 minutes. Cool in the liquid, strain, discarding the shells. Use shrimp flavored broth as a base for soups, chowders and sauces. Freeze for up to six months.

Always fluff your cooked rice with a fork. The fork allows steam to escape leaving your rice fluffy.

When boiling corn on the cob, add a pinch of sugar to help bring out the corn's natural sweetness.

To prevent eggshells from cracking, add a pinch of salt to the water before hard-boiling.

NO TIME TO COOK

In cooking, as in all the arts,
simplicity is the sign of perfection.
Maurice-Edmond Sailland

NO TIME TO COOK

We know how fortunate we are to be such good girlfriends and to have the resources to get away together at least twice a year and indulge in the extreme, the ridiculous, and sometimes the absolutely outrageous. Most of the time, however, we are business women, wives, and mothers, committed to maintaining the continuity of the workplace and our homes. Dependability is the cornerstone of our lives, and we've noticed that sometimes the consistency of our routines can get rather boring.

For us, it is always delightful to discover a new recipe and experiment with the ingredients. It is not always so delightful to prepare the old tried-and-true that our children and our spouses tend to prefer on a daily basis. This collection of menus and recipes came out of a discussion among the Fabulous Five concerning the sometimes tedious yet important responsibilities of routine cooking. We concluded that we should just save our epicurean exuberance for special occasions and give our families what they want with the least effort possible. Each of us has contributed our quickest and easiest family favorites to this chapter, and we are confident these menus will satisfy the tired and hungry without taxing the time and spirit of the creative cook.

Green Chili Corn Bread
Cajun Shrimp and Corn Bisque
Mammaw's Chocolate Pie

GREEN CHILI CORN BREAD

1½	sticks unsalted butter, room temperature
1	cup yellow cornmeal
6	T. sugar
4	large eggs
1½	cups all purpose flour
1	T. baking powder
1¼	t. salt
1	15 oz. can cream style corn
1	4 oz. can diced green chilies
⅓	cup cheddar cheese
⅓	cup grated Monterey Jack cheese

Yield: 9 servings

Preheat oven to 375°. Lightly oil 9 inch square baking pan. Using an electric mixer; beat butter, cornmeal and sugar in large bowl until well blended. Add eggs 1 at a time, beating well after each addition. Mix flour, baking powder and salt in small bowl. Add to batter and stir well. Mix in corn, chilies and both cheeses. Pour batter into prepared pan. Bake until tester inserted into center comes out clean, about 45 minutes. Cool slightly. Cut into squares.

CAJUN SHRIMP AND CORN BISQUE

Very tasty – very easy!

4	cups fat-free milk
2	cups diced peeled potatoes
1	t. Cajun seasoning
¼	t. salt
¼	t. pepper
2	14 oz. cans cream-style corn
1	lb. large shrimp, peeled and deveined

Yield: 4 servings

Combine the first five ingredients in a Dutch oven and bring to a boil. (Do this slowly or your pan will look like mine does now.) Reduce heat, and simmer the milk mixture for 10 minutes, stirring occasionally. Stir in the corn and bring to a boil. Add the shrimp and cook for 2 minutes or until shrimp are done.

MAMMAW'S CHOCOLATE PIE

Best chocolate pie ever! From the best Mammaw ever!

1¾	cups sugar
9¾	T. flour
3	egg yolks (save whites for meringue)
5½	T. cocoa
1¾	cups milk
1½	T. butter
¾	t. vanilla
	pie shell (store bought)

Yield: 6-8 servings

Cook the pie shell according to instructions. Set aside.

Cook first five ingredients on medium heat, stirring occasionally at first, then constant as the pudding thickens. Cook until thick. Add the butter and vanilla.

Pour into cooked pie shell. Whip egg whites until stiff (can add 4 to 5 T. of sugar if desired). Top pie with meringue then brown meringue.

"I like mine room temperature, Jeff loves his cold. This pie will not stay around long either way. Promise the "pan" to the one you love (that day)."

Watermelon and Avocado Salad
Parmesan Chicken Fingers
Creamy Veggie Pasta
Jodi's Rich Chocolate Trifle

WATERMELON AND AVOCADO SALAD

1	small red onion, peeled and sliced very thinly
2	T. red-wine vinegar
2	ripe avocados
	juice of 1 lime
¼	large watermelon (about 6 pounds)
	juice of 1 orange
2	t. extra virgin olive oil
1	cup cilantro sprigs, loosely packed
	salt and pepper (to taste)

Yield: 6 Servings

In a small bowl, combine onion and vinegar. Marinate, covered, in refrigerator for several hours or overnight.

Cut avocados in half, remove pits and skin. Cut into 1 inch chunks and toss with the lime juice. Remove seeds from watermelon and cut into 1½ inch chunks.

Toss together watermelon, avocado, orange juice, olive oil and cilantro sprigs, reserving some sprigs for garnish. Drain onion and vinegar mixture and add to salad; add salt and pepper to taste. Toss again and garnish with reserved cilantro.

"When one has tasted watermelons, one knows what Angels eat."

Mark Twain

PARMESAN CHICKEN FINGERS

Great for quick meal. Very tasty.

12 chicken tenders, thawed
1 egg, beaten
1 cup parmesan cheese
1 cup herbed bread crumbs

Yield: 3 or 4 servings

Preheat oven to 375°.

Rinse chicken tenders. Mix parmesan cheese and bread crumbs. Roll chicken in egg then cheese and breadcrumb mixture. Place on greased jelly roll pan. Bake 18-20 minutes. Turn chicken and bake 2 to 3 more minutes. Serve plain or with honey.

CREAMY VEGGIE PASTA

½ package frozen mixed vegetables
½ cup plain yogurt
¼-½ cup Picanté sauce
½ package Rotini pasta
2 t. garlic powder
salt and pepper (to taste)

Yield: 4 servings

Boil the vegetables as directed. Drain. (You can also boil your pasta with the veggies!) Add all other ingredients. Heat to serve.

"Never eat more than you can lift."

Miss Piggy

JODI'S RICH CHOCOLATE TRIFLE

This recipe is quick and easy but you will want to make parts of this dessert ahead.

1	chocolate fudge cake mix (prepared)
1	6 oz. instant chocolate pudding (prepared)
12	oz. Cool Whip
½	cup strong coffee, brewed
6	full sized Toffee Bars, Heath or Skor bars, chopped

Yield: 8-10 servings

Bake cake according to instructions. Make pudding according to instructions. (May want to bake the cake and mix the pudding the night before serving.) Cool completely. Crumble the cake and save ½ cup to use as topping, along with ½ cup of the toffee pieces. Place half of the cake crumbles into the bottom of a trifle dish and pour ½ of the coffee over it to saturate. Layer ½ of the pudding, cool whip and toffee. Repeat. Combine the ½ cup of cake with the ½ cup of toffee pieces to sprinkle on the very top. Chill at least 4 to 5 hours.

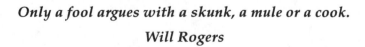

Only a fool argues with a skunk, a mule or a cook.

Will Rogers

Banana Pineapple Salad
Rebe's Roast Dinner
Easy Fruit Cobbler

BANANA PINEAPPLE SALAD

2	bananas
1	4 oz. can of pineapple chunks, drained
1	T. mayonnaise
1	T. sugar (optional)

Slice the bananas in a bowl. Add the pineapple chunks. Stir the mayonnaise and sugar (if desired) into the salad and serve immediately.

REBE'S ROAST DINNER

Most tender roast ever.

2	lbs. chuck roast
1	can cream of mushroom soup
2	cans green beans (do not drain)
3	potatoes, quartered
4	carrots, peel and sliced
1	onion, quartered

Yield: 6 servings

Put roast in covered roasting pan. Add can of cream of mushroom soup, green beans with juice. Cut up potatoes, carrots and onion. Add all these to the roast. Bake on 300° for 3-4 hours. (I always put out frozen rolls and bake to be ready at the same time.)

EASY FRUIT COBBLER

Mix together:

¾   cup flour
¾   cup sugar
1½ t. baking powder
½   cup milk
1   can fruit filling
     (your choice)

½   cup butter

Yield: 8-10 servings

In 350° oven melt ½ cup butter in a 9 × 13 cake pan.

Pour mixture into melted butter and top with canned fruit filling of choice (do not stir). Bake until brown about 30 minutes. Vanilla ice cream and chopped pecans optional.

*"There is no love sincerer than
the love of food."*

George Bernard Shaw

Autumn Green Bean Salad
Layered Herbed Chicken
Strawberry Pie

AUTUMN GREEN BEAN SALAD

Vinaigrette:
¼ cup orange juice
¼ cup white wine vinegar
2 T. water
2 t. vegetable oil
1 t. prepared horseradish
1 t. honey
1 t. Dijon mustard
¼ t. black pepper

Salad:
1½ lbs. green beans, trimmed
1 cup vertically sliced red onion
1 cup oranges, slices
1 cup seedless red grapes, halved

Yield: 6-8 servings

To prepare vinaigrette, combine first 8 ingredients in a jar, cover tightly and shake vigorously. Chill.

To prepare salad, steam the green beans, covered 3 minutes or until tender, and chill. Combine green beans, onion slices, orange slices and grape halves in a large bowl. Drizzle vinaigrette over salad, tossing gently to coat.

So whether you eat or drink, or whatever you do, do all to the glory of God.

1 Corinthians 10:31

LAYERED HERBED CHICKEN

4-6 boneless chicken breast
1 can cream of chicken soup
4-6 slices of Swiss cheese
1 box or package of herbed seasoned stuffing mix
¼ cup butter, melted

Yield: 4-6 servings

Lay the boneless chicken breast flat in a baking dish. Pour the cream of chicken soup over chicken. Lay slices of Swiss cheese on top and sprinkle with the herbed seasoned stuffing mix. Pour the butter over and bake at 350° for 30 to 45 minutes uncovered.

STRAWBERRY PIE

1 quart strawberries, washed and cut
2 cups boiling water
1 small box strawberry gelatin
4 T. cornstarch
2 cups sugar
pie crust, baked
whipping cream (optional)

Yield: 6-8 servings

Mix ingredients well. Cook for 6 minutes. Cool thoroughly. Place In prebaked pie crust. Top with strawberries and whipped cream.

Classic Waldorf Salad
Gee Gee's Delicious Chicken
Brown Rice Almondine
Easy Praline Bars

CLASSIC WALDORF SALAD

½   cup mayonnaise
1   T. sugar
1   T. lemon juice
⅛   t. salt
3   medium apples, diced
1   cup sliced celery
½   cup chopped walnuts

Yield: 5½ cups

Combine first four ingredients. Stir in remaining ingredients. Cover, chill well.

GEE GEE'S DELICIOUS CHICKEN

6-8   chicken thighs
2   cans of tomato soup
2   T. Worcestershire Sauce
4   T. vinegar
4   T. butter
4   T. sweet pickle relish
½   small onion, chopped

Yield: 4-6 servings

Brown chicken in the butter. Mix the remaining ingredients, pour over the chicken and simmer until done. Flip the chicken a couple of times and cover with mixture during cooking. About 45 minutes.

Serve over Brown Rice Almondine.

BROWN RICE ALMONDINE

1	medium onion, chopped
2	t. butter
1¼	cups chicken broth
1	T. lemon juice
½	t. garlic powder
1½	cups instant brown rice
1	cup frozen cut green beans, thawed
2	T. sliced almonds, toasted
½	t. dill weed

Yield: 6 servings

Cook and stir onion in hot butter until tender. Add broth, lemon juice and garlic powder. Bring to boil.

Stir in rice. Return to boil. Reduce heat to low; cover and simmer 5 minutes. Remove from heat.

Stir in green beans, almonds and dill; cover. Let stand 5 minutes.

EASY PRALINE BARS

12	whole graham crackers
1	cup brown sugar
1	stick butter
1	cup chopped nuts

Yield: 12 large bars or 24 smaller bars

Boil sugar and butter for 3 minutes. Place graham crackers in a jelly roll pan. Pour mixture over crackers. Sprinkle nuts on top. Bake 10 minutes at 350°. Watch closely, not to burn. Cool and break into bars.

Chicken Caesar Salad
Quickest Crescent Roll Bread
Easy Lemon Squares

CHICKEN CAESAR SALAD

Leftover cooked boneless
    chicken (for the quick
    and easiest)
head of romaine lettuce
parmesan cheese, fresh grated
    is best, optional
whole wheat bread (or store
    bought croutons)

Dressing:
½   cup olive oil
1   garlic clove, finely minced
Blend together in blender.
    Reserve about 2 T. to
    use on croutons.

Add to mixture:
½   t. salt
¼   t. ground mustard
¼   t. black pepper
dash of Worcestershire sauce
1   hard-boiled egg
1   T. lemon juice
2   T. red wine vinegar

Blend together.

Yield: 4 servings

To make croutons:

Cut whole-wheat bread into cubes: pour reserve oil/garlic mixture over cubes and broil until browned on all sides.

Break up romaine lettuce and cover each plate. Cut chicken in small pieces and place on top of lettuce. Sprinkle with croutons and drizzle dressing over all and sprinkle with grated parmesan cheese.

Footnote: When you barbecue, cook extra boneless chicken breast and freeze. They are great to use in this salad. To thaw out, put a small amount of water in a sauce pan. Make a bowl out of foil and place chicken in bowl and put in a pan. Cover and steam until chicken is thawed out.

QUICKEST CRESCENT ROLL BREAD

Comes out like a cake. Delicious and simple!

½   cup butter
3   packages crescent rolls

Yield: 8-10 servings

Preheat oven to 350°. Melt butter in bundt pan. Place 3 packages of crescent rolls end to end (without unrolling) in pan in butter. Bake about 45 minutes.

Turn out on a plate like you would a cake.

EASY LEMON SQUARES

Crust:
¼   cup sugar
3   T. butter, softened
1   cup flour

Topping:
3   large eggs
¾   cup sugar
2   t. lemon rind, grated
⅓   cup fresh lemon juice
3   T. flour
½   t. baking powder
⅛   t. salt
2   t. powdered sugar

Yield: 16 servings

Preheat oven to 350°. To prepare the crust, beat ¼ cup sugar and the butter at medium speed with a mixer until creamy. Lightly spoon 1 cup flour into a dry measuring cup; level with a knife. Gradually add 1 cup flour to sugar until mixture resembles fine crumbs. Gently press mixture into bottom of an 8 inch square baking pan. Bake at 350° for 15 minutes; cool on a wire rack.

To prepare topping, beat eggs at medium speed until foamy. Add ¾ cup sugar and next 5 ingredients , and beat until well-blended. Pour mixture over partially baked crust. Bake at 350° for 20 to 25 minutes or until set. Cool on wire rack. Sift powdered sugar evenly over top.

Crisp Green Salad with Vinaigrette
Crock Pot Meal
Quick Chocolate Mousse

CRISP GREEN SALAD WITH VINAIGRETTE

8   leaves romaine lettuce
1   small head curly endive
1   small head Belgian endive

Vinaigrette:
2   T. oil
2   t. red wine vinegar
½   t. Dijon mustard
salt and pepper to taste

Yield: 4 servings

Wash and dry the greens, tear into bite size pieces and place in a bowl. Combine oil, vinegar, mustard, salt and pepper in a jar. Cover and shake well. Drizzle the dressing over the greens, toss and serve.

CROCK POT MEAL

4-6   chicken breast or pork chops
1   onion, sliced
1   can cream of mushroom soup
3   potatoes (cubed)
salt and pepper to taste

Yield: 4 servings

Rinse the meat well and put in crock pot. Add the sliced onion, cream of mushroom soup, potato cubes and salt and pepper. Cook all day on low.

248

QUICK CHOCOLATE MOUSSE

Fast, easy, delicious.

1   can Eagle brand milk
1   small package chocolate
     pudding mix
1   cup cold water
2   cups Cool Whip

Yield: 4-6 servings

In large mixing bowl beat all ingredients except Cool Whip. Chill 5 minutes.

Fold in 2 cups Cool Whip. Chill until ready to serve.

*"A good cook is like a sorceress
who dispenses happiness."*

Elsa

Cranberry and Orange Salad
Easy Pork Chops
Blueberry Pudding

CRANBERRY AND ORANGE SALAD

1-1½ packages of assorted greens
1-1½ packages dried
    cranberries
1   cup walnuts, chopped
1   medium purple onion,
    chopped
1   can mandarin oranges,
    drained
1   small bottle fat free
    vinaigrette dressing

Yield: 4 servings

Mix all the ingredients and stir in dressing just before serving.

EASY PORK CHOPS

Good job Deb! Love these.

1   package pork chops
    (thin sliced)
¼   cup Lite Teriyaki Sauce
½   package cole slaw mix
    (prepackaged)
1   small package frozen peas
    or corn
garlic powder
orange (optional)

Yield: 4-6 servings

Spray a non-stick fry pan and sauté pork chops until lightly browned. Add the cole slaw, vegetable, teriyaki sauce and spices. Cover and simmer for about 20 minutes. Serve over rice.

BLUEBERRY PUDDING

1   16 oz. package frozen
     unsweetened blueberries
     (about 4 cups)
¾   cup firmly packed golden
     brown sugar
1   T. plus 1 cup all purpose
     flour
½   cup chilled unsalted
     butter, diced
1   cup milk
1   egg
2   t. grated lemon peel
½   t. vanilla extract
vanilla ice cream (optional)

Yield: 6-8 servings

Preheat oven to 350°. Grease 9 inch glass pie dish. Place frozen berries in bowl. Add ¼ cup brown sugar and 1 T. flour, toss to coat berries. Spoon mixture into prepared pie dish. In medium bowl, rub remaining 1 cup flour and butter together with fingertips until coarse meal forms. Mix in remaining ½ cup brown sugar. Add milk, egg, lemon peel and vanilla; stir to blend. Pour batter over berry mixture. Bake pudding until center is firm and top is golden brown, about 55 minutes. Let cool 10 minutes. Spoon into deep dessert bowls, top with ice cream if desired.

"There is no sight on earth more appealing than the sight of a woman making dinner for someone she loves."

Thomas Wolf

Melba's Layered Peach Dessert
Easy Swiss Quiche
Zucchini Medley

MELBA'S LAYERED PEACH DESSERT

¼	cup sugar
3	cups fresh peaches, chopped
1½	cups flour
¼	cup firmly packed brown sugar
½	cup chopped pecans
½	cup butter or margarine, melted
1	8 oz. package cream cheese, softened
1¾	cups sifted powdered sugar
1	8 oz. container frozen whipped topping, thawed
¼-½	t. almond extract

Yield: 15 servings

Sprinkle sugar over the chopped peaches, stir gently and let stand 30 minutes.

Combine flour, brown sugar and pecans in a medium bowl; stir in butter. Press into bottom of 13 × 9 × 2 inch baking dish.

Bake at 350° for 18 to 20 minutes. Cool crust on a wire rack.

Combine cream cheese and powdered sugar and beat at medium speed with an electric mixer until fluffy. Fold in whipped topping and almond extract.

Drain peaches, discarding the liquid. Fold peaches into cream cheese mixture. Spoon over the crust, spreading evenly. Cover and chill 3 to 4 hours.

EASY SWISS QUICHE

1	unbaked pie shell
¾	cup milk
2	eggs
½	t. salt
½	t. pepper
¼	t. garlic salt
Dry onions to taste	
½	t. chives
1	small can mushroom pieces
1½	cups swiss cheese, grated
2	T. flour

Toss cheese with 2 tablespoons flour. Beat milk and eggs. Mix all ingredients and pour into unbaked pie shell. Bake at 325° for 1 hour or until set.

ZUCCHINI MEDLEY

1	small onion, chopped
1	T. butter
2	medium zucchini, sliced
½	cup water
1	package frozen whole-kernel corn
1	large tomato, diced

Yield: 4 servings

Sauté the onion in the butter. Add the 2 sliced zucchinis and the water, cover and simmer for 10 minutes. Add the diced tomato and simmer just until tomato is hot. (There should not be much liquid in the pan when tomatoes are added to be certain of maximum flavor.)

(Also goes well with fish or chicken)

Chunky Avocado and Tomato Salad
Hamburger Corn Pone
Ice Cream Sundae Cake

CHUNKY AVOCADO AND TOMATO SALAD

4	large ripe avocado's, cut into 1" cubes
4	large tomatoes, cut into 1" pieces
1	cup cottage cheese (½ cup more if you prefer)
2-3	t. garlic salt

Yield: 4 servings

Combine all of the ingredients and refrigerate at least 1 hour.

HAMBURGER CORN PONE

Old family favorite

1	lb. ground beef
2	t. chili powder
1	t. Worcestershire sauce
1	can kidney beans, drained
⅓	cup chopped onion
¾	t. salt
1	can chopped tomatoes
	cornbread batter (packaged mix prepared according to directions)

Yield: 4-6 servings

Brown the meat and chopped onion. Add seasonings and the tomatoes. Simmer for 15 minutes. Add kidney beans and pour into greased casserole dish. Top with cornbread batter, spreading evenly and not too thick. Bake in oven at 450° until bread is cooked (see packaged mix cook time. Approximately 20 minutes).

ICE CREAM SUNDAE CAKE

Set out to soften:
½   gallon vanilla ice cream
     (rectangle shaped box
     works best)

Melt together:
1   stick butter
1   cup packed brown sugar

Add:
2½   cups crushed Rice Chex
1   cup coconut
½   cup chopped pecans
chocolate syrup (optional)

Yield: 10-12 servings

Place ½ of the cereal mixture on the bottom of pan (11" × 13" or 12" × 12"). Slice ice cream with a large knife into approximately 4 even slices (a liberal inch). Place ice cream in pan using a large spatula to "spread" the softened ice cream filling in between the gaps with the more melted ice cream. Top with the remaining cereal mixture. Refreeze till ready to serve. Soften a few moments before serving: Individual servings may be topped with chocolate syrup.

FAB FIVE FOOTNOTES

A clever wife found out how to remove cooking odors from the house—she quit cooking.

For fluffy mashed potatoes: Always warm your milk first. Even better melt your butter with the milk then add to the potatoes and mash.

Try sprinkling Parmesan cheese or soy sauce on your popcorn for a healthy, low-calorie snack.

For a cracker substitute, slice bagels paper-thin and toast with butter and herbs. Great to eat crisp with salads and cheese.

To make cheese easy to grate: freeze 15 minutes prior to grating.

Poke holes in potatoes with an aluminum skewer—they will bake quicker.

Fresh garlic: you can clean a bunch of bulbs of garlic and store the cloves in a tightly covered jar full of olive oil. The oil preserves the garlic for months and is heavenly to use in cooking.

Powdered milk should always be kept on hand for times when you run out of milk.

Pour oil and vinegar into the remains on the bottom of a ketchup bottle. Shake vigorously to make a great salad dressing.

Cake coating: For a quick, delicious icing, spread warmed honey over cake and sprinkle with chopped nuts or grated coconut.

Handy potatoes: Boil a few extras and have in refrigerator for a quick dish. Makes good potato salad. Slice for scalloped or grate for hash browns.

Fast seasoning: Keep a large shaker with salt and pepper mixed (six parts salt to one part pepper).

SEASON YOUR FRIENDSHIPS

Girlfriends Talk Back

I have four very close girlfriends that have a wonderful history. We call ourselves the "Fabulous Five" because, well, we are. ... What started out as cooking together on a monthly basis in Lubbock 11 years ago has blossomed into a traveling, eating, cooking, sharing extravaganza. We've been through births, deaths, cancer, career moves, etc., and have come through it a much stronger, more spiritual group of women. Every year we take a trip together where we pamper ourselves, shop, eat, visit, eat and play catch up with each other's lives; and every year we get a little "deeper" with our thoughts, prayers and hopes for each other. I couldn't have made it through a few tough years without my girlfriends. We are blessed to have each other.

The Fabulous Five: From left, Jan Tonroy, Diane Earl, Debbie Rubin, Stephanie McKee, Phyllis Jones

— *Debbie Rubin*

We actually made the news! Girlfriends are a trendy topic these days, and we are proud to have been best friends for so long, we can claim to be way ahead of the times. We can also claim that we will most definitely remain best friends long after this fine topic leaves the front page!

Creating this cookbook has been our shared labor of love, with the extra benefit of giving us a gratifying justification for organizing our Fall Retreat each year. We hope our sharing of recipes and life stories will inspire you to realize there is "always enough 'thyme' for great friends, fabulous food, and spirited fun." We encourage you to season your friendships with special traditions and spectacular entertainments. Plan meals together. Go for weekend outings. Make the "thyme" to build deep bonds and celebrate the richness of life.

The Fall Retreat is now an established tradition, and we are already brainstorming ideas and collecting recipes for our next "celebration of food and friendship." We would love to add your girlfriend adventures to our forthcoming publication. Please share your stories of friendship with us. Send pictures and tales to:

The Fabulous Five, Inc.
P.O. Box 1068
Aledo, Texas 76008
Email: Fabfive54321@aol.com
Fax: (817) 441-5032

The Fabulous Five

RENEE STEGER SIMPSON

We are proud to feature the cover art of Lubbock artist Renee Steger Simpson and join Simpson's ever growing watercolor series entitled "Snooty Women." Besides creating art and exhibiting in Taos, New Mexico and Lubbock, Texas, Simpson is a professional accountant. The Snooty Women Series grew out of a combination of professional relationships that began to germinate in her art in October of 1992, beginning with a few intuitive marks that quickly evolved into a form revealing her ironic feelings about particular people and situations. As of the year 2001, Simpson has been inspired to create over 85 watercolors in the series with most now on display in private as well as corporate collections.

Simpson was raised in an artistic family. Her grandfather and mother were prolific painters, and the family spent a great deal of time in and around Taos, New Mexico, an environment that has been a continuous source of inspiration for her life and art. Simpson is as inspired by the New Mexico landscape and way of life as she is by the complicated personalities of women and also paints bold watercolors on topics and themes Southwest, as well as vibrantly expressive florals. She has had a love of watercolor since high school and continues to celebrate the medium for its infinite surprises. "I work primarily in watercolor," she explains, "because the unpredictability and challenge of the medium coincides with all of my expectations of creativity. Something exciting always happens."

Today, Simpson divides her time between her private accounting practice and her art, often traveling to New Mexico to paint on location in Taos. In 2000, Simpson's watercolor *Got Harley?* was juried into the Texas Watercolor Society's 51st annual traveling exhibit. She is represented in Taos, New Mexico, by Bryan's Gallery and exhibits in galleries throughout Lubbock, Texas, including participation in numerous juries exhibitions by the Lubbock Art Association and One Woman Shows at Llano Estacado Winery.

INDEX

E

F

To Order *Always Enough Thyme*

Please send _____ copies @ $21.95 (U.S.) each $ _____

Plus postage and handling @ $3.50 each $ _____

Texas residents add sales tax @ $1.48 each $ _____

Check or Credit Card (Canada-credit card only) TOTAL $ _____

Charge to my: ☐ MasterCard or ☐ VISA

Account # _____

Expiration date _____

Signature _____

> **Fabulous Five, Inc.**
> **P.O. Box 1068**
> **Aledo, TX 76008**
> **FAX OR CALL:**
> **(817) 441-5032**

Name _____

Address _____

City _____ State _____ Zip _____

Phone (day) _____ (night) _____

For more information, please fax to: Fabulous Five, Inc. at (817) 441-5032

To Order *Always Enough Thyme*

Please send _____ copies @ $21.95 (U.S.) each $ _____

Plus postage and handling @ $3.50 each $ _____

Texas residents add sales tax @ $1.48 each $ _____

Check or Credit Card (Canada-credit card only) TOTAL $ _____

Charge to my: ☐ MasterCard or ☐ VISA

Account # _____

Expiration date _____

Signature _____

> **Fabulous Five, Inc.**
> **P.O. Box 1068**
> **Aledo, TX 76008**
> **FAX OR CALL:**
> **(817) 441-5032**

Name _____

Address _____

City _____ State _____ Zip _____

Phone (day) _____ (night) _____

For more information, please fax to: Fabulous Five, Inc. at (817) 441-5032

To Order *Always Enough Thyme*

Please send _____ copies @ $21.95 (U.S.) each $ _____

Plus postage and handling @ $3.50 each $ _____

Texas residents add sales tax @ $1.48 each $ _____

Check or Credit Card (Canada-credit card only) TOTAL $ _____

Charge to my: ☐ MasterCard or ☐ VISA

Account # _____

Expiration date _____

Signature _____

Fabulous Five, Inc.
P.O. Box 1068
Aledo, TX 76008
FAX OR CALL:
(817) 441-5032

Name _____

Address _____

City _____ State _____ Zip _____

Phone (day) _____ (night) _____

For more information, please fax to: Fabulous Five, Inc. at (817) 441-5032

To Order *Always Enough Thyme*

Please send _____ copies @ $21.95 (U.S.) each $ _____

Plus postage and handling @ $3.50 each $ _____

Texas residents add sales tax @ $1.48 each $ _____

Check or Credit Card (Canada-credit card only) TOTAL $ _____

Charge to my: ☐ MasterCard or ☐ VISA

Account # _____

Expiration date _____

Signature _____

Fabulous Five, Inc.
P.O. Box 1068
Aledo, TX 76008
FAX OR CALL:
(817) 441-5032

Name _____

Address _____

City _____ State _____ Zip _____

Phone (day) _____ (night) _____

For more information, please fax to: Fabulous Five, Inc. at (817) 441-5032